BLAZING GUNS, WILD HORSES, & THE GRACE OF GOD

THE JAMES KILPATRICK STORY

Dana Maria Hill

authorHOUSE®

AuthorHouse™
1663 Liberty Drive
Bloomington, IN 47403
www.authorhouse.com
Phone: 1-800-839-8640

First published by AuthorHouse 5/2/2011

ISBN: 978-1-4567-4396-3 (e)
ISBN: 978-1-4567-4397-0 (hc)
ISBN: 978-1-4567-4398-7 (sc)

Library of Congress Control Number: 2011903913

Printed in the United States of America

The People History – www.thepeoplehistory.com
Parkinson.org
The National Institute of Neurological Disorders and Strokes
Scripture quotations marked "KJV" are taken from the King James Version of the
Holy Bible © 1989 Thomas Nelson, Inc. Used by permission. All rights reserved.
This book is printed on acid-free paper.

This book is dedicated to the memory of:

James David Kilpatrick (5/27/1934–11/25/2009)

Aubrey Kilpatrick (2/22/1912–5/17/1951)

Elizabeth Kilpatrick (10/29/1913–9/3/1990)

Jeretta Kilpatrick Scott (9/1/1938–8/4/2009)

Daniel Columbus Kilpatrick (1/14/1950–5/25/2006)

Infant son of Aubrey and Elizabeth Kilpatrick (9/2/1951–9/2/1951)

CONTENTS

ACKNOWLEDGMENTS

A heartfelt thanks to my Heavenly Father for giving me the insight and inspiration to write this story.

A special thanks to Ann Kilpatrick for all the long hours she worked on this project and, most of all, for believing in me and giving me this opportunity. I admire you for your loyalty and love to your husband and for allowing me the honor of remembering him.

To Marty and Rhonda Kilpatrick, thank you for allowing me to pick at your heart and open up those raw emotions over and over again. I could not have finished this book without your support and encouragement. Marty, your photographic memory is amazing! Thank you for sharing all those wonderful stories that your dad shared with you.

To my pastor, Brother Wayne White, thank you for continued prayer, encouragement, and support on this project. I love the gentleness of your heart.

To all the friends and members of the Kilpatrick family, thank you from the bottom of my heart. It was such an honor to share sweet fellowship with you and to hear all the stories. You made me laugh and cry at the same time. The thoughts you shared about Brother James have turned this story into a memorial.

ABOUT THE BOOK

This is the story of one man's amazing journey, his destination, and the intervention of an almighty God.

The tragic event of May 17, 1951, changed the lives of many families forever. Numerous newspaper articles have been written about that night and what took place, but this story is different from anything that was ever printed. This is the event as it happened through the eyes of a sixteen-year-old boy, watching as his father was gunned down and died in front of him.

James Kilpatrick escaped the hand of death, dodging bullets and standing strong and brave to protect his family. The enemy sought to destroy him, but God sent angels to camp around him and protect him. That night began a long, hard journey to places unknown and dangers unseen.

Come walk with me through these pages as we pull back the curtain and view the life and testimony of James David Kilpatrick.

INTRODUCTION

There are two sides to every story and then there is the truth. "The God of heaven is the truth and He can not lie." (Titus 1:2 KJV)

May 17, 1951, was a dreadful day for everyone involved. The events of that night will forever be etched in my mind. Many families were devastated, and everyone walked away a loser. So many precious lives were lost. Wives lost husbands, children lost fathers, mothers lost sons, and I lost my youth and innocence. A community mourned its fallen. I wish I could forget; but, try as I may, the picture is as clear as the day it happened, and the hurt still pierces my heart. Not a day goes by that I don't remember. I desperately wanted things to turn out differently that night.

Many years have passed since the day my life changed forever. I often think about all the families that were involved, and the outcome. As I reflect on where I was, where I've been, and where I'm going, I can't help but get excited. It thrills me that God in all his goodness reached down and saved a lost sinner like me. I gave my heart and life to Jesus, and he restored my soul. He lifted me out of the pits of hell and broke my chains. He set my feet on a firm foundation. His grace, mercy, and love changed my life forever. Life is hard, but God is faithful. We live and learn.

Would I go back and change things that have happened in my life? Yes; if given the chance, we all would. But the truth is, we can't go back, so we must move forward.

"When I was a child, I spake as a child, I understood as a child, I thought as a child: but when I became a man, I put away childish things." (1 Cor. 13:11 KJV)

This is my story . . .

CHAPTER ONE:
CHILDHOOD DAYS

THE YEAR WAS 1932, a time of economic hardship. Many farmers were forced from their homes that year. Thirteen million Americans were out of work. In November, American voters used their power of democracy and voted in Franklin D. Roosevelt as president. Times were changing. A young, ambitious man by the name of Aubrey Evelyn Kilpatrick wed Nellie Elizabeth Pankey on December 16, 1932. The wedding took place in Sardis, Alabama, a small town on top of Sand Mountain just northeast of Birmingham. My parents had eight children. My name is James David Kilpatrick, and I am the oldest.

I was raised by a father who welcomed hard work with open arms and a mother who loved her family. She stood beside her husband through good times and bad, whether he was right or wrong. Daddy was well versed in a number of trades. He could break any high-spirited horse, and he could rope and ride better than any cowboy I ever knew. Aubrey Kilpatrick was an excellent marksman. He also distributed some of the finest white lightning in the South.

Moonshine was hauled to our farm from the mountains of Tennessee in the back of a 1933 Ford. It was delivered to us in containers, and then we poured it into bottles. As a child, I would get falling-down drunk from smelling it, but I never drank the stuff. Mother made some of the best peach syrup on the mountain. She would mix the syrup with moonshine and let it blend for a while. It was our most-requested "recipe" and a favorite with the locals. I had a fast pony that I rode to deliver moonshine, and nobody could catch me on that pony. The moonshine business was a family affair and brought in a secure income. Bootlegging was a thriving business in those days. The law didn't take too kindly to us selling moonshine illegally in a dry county. Some corrupt law officers would force the local bootleggers to pay them off, and, of course, that money went into their own pockets. There was and still is corruption on all levels of politics. Daddy refused to pay his dues and quickly made enemies in high places. Trouble was brewing.

Daddy was a landowner with several tenant farmers living and working on his land. He owned land in Marshall and Dekalb Counties in northern Alabama. Some of the farmers who worked on our land were rough, rowdy, and mean. Their generation had been beaten down from the Great Depression, and they were trying to survive. Times were hard for them, and often they turned to drinking for relief. It helped them to escape the pressures of life and all their problems for a little while. My daddy was compassionate to people who were down on their luck. The Great Depression had left a bitter taste in their mouths, and they were still feeling the effects.

Daddy was as high-spirited as any horse he ever broke. He had a fiery temper, and he feared no man. He was not a churchgoing man, but he had respect for the church and the community where we lived. Daddy was quick to help anyone and would give you the shirt off his back. Preacher Minor had to walk to church every Sunday, and when Daddy found out about it, he gave him a mule to ride to church. Aubrey Kilpatrick had a heart the size of Texas. Whenever a neighbor would fall sick and wasn't able to work, Daddy would take us boys to plow, plant, and harvest his crops until he was back on his feet. "Good neighbors take care of each other," he would say. I can't tell you how many times I heard that growing up. That man loved his community and his neighbors.

Mr. Harvey Roebuck lived in the Union community where I grew up. The Kilpatrick family had nothing but respect for him. He had a large pond that was used by the local churches for baptizing folks. One year, a bad storm came through, and lightning struck the dam. Mr. Roebuck needed help, and Daddy was the first man to volunteer. He took his best team of horses, Jess and Duke, and worked diligently to rebuild the dam. All the men in the community pitched in. Most of the men would use a line on their horses, but not Daddy. Jess and Duke would follow the other horses. One man would load dirt into a bucket, and another would unload it. Jess and Duke were well behaved and properly trained. The dam was rebuilt in no time at all. Aubrey Kilpatrick earned the respect of the community. If he was your friend, you had a friend for life, and he would do anything he could to help you.

Mr. Watts was another local farmer who lived in our community. He had been working endlessly with a dual-wheel tractor to remove some large logs from the creek. Needless to say, he was having no luck. The logs were too heavy for the tractor to pull out without turning over. When Daddy found out, he hooked chains to Jess and Duke, and they pulled every log out of that creek. They would go four or five steps at a time and then repeat it over and over until the task was completed. They were big, strong horses, and they obeyed my father's command. They feared and respected him, just as I did.

Daddy loved children and had a heart for the fatherless. A child could melt that tough-guy image in a heartbeat. A local boy named Marlon had lost his dad at the age of five. He was a friend to me and my brother Billy. Marlon's mom, Mrs. Effie, was a godly woman who struggled to make ends meet. Aubrey Kilpatrick thought it was a shame that the boy didn't have a horse, so he gave Marlon a pony and a bag of feed. He taught him to ride, and he told him to ride it well. Daddy also provided wire for a hog pen, a hog, and a bag of feed for Mrs. Effie and her family. He was a father figure to many young boys and a good neighbor to everyone. Marlon ate many meals at our home and spent the night with us often. He was like one of the family. Another kid named Fred Howard Burns actually lived with us. His mom was terminally ill, and his dad was a taxi driver who worked late hours. Mr. Burns asked Daddy if Fred could come live with us, because he wasn't able to take care of him. Daddy agreed, and Fred Howard Burns moved in.

Mother never seemed to mind that there was always a full house for supper. She had lots of patience and was one of the finest cooks on Sand Mountain. Big biscuits with chocolate syrup was a favorite recipe. When she prepared a meal, it was enough to feed an army. Almost every Saturday, we would saddle up the horses and ride into town. Daddy would ride Jess, and Mother would ride Duke. We would stop at several houses on the way and gather up some of the neighborhood kids to ride in with us. Daddy would treat us all to a candy bar and a Coca-Cola. That was almost as good as a banana sandwich in those days. Children were drawn to my father. He was a charitable man, but that was not to be confused with weakness. If you crossed him, there would be consequences.

One of Daddy's brothers, Veston, was married to a good, godly woman named Polly. Aunt Polly would not tolerate drinking. When Uncle Veston would go out drinking with Daddy and the boys, they would pull up beside the house and roll him out of the car because they were afraid of Aunt Polly. No one wanted to deal with her wrath! Uncle Veston liked to drink, and one night at a ballgame he had too much to drink. The law arrested him for public intoxication and hauled him off to jail. While he was there, one of the police officers roughed him up. When Daddy found out, he rounded up some of us boys, and we paid a visit to the police station. Daddy had words with the officer, and some threats were made. That policeman left town that night and never returned to Marshall County. You did not want to mess with Aubrey Kilpatrick, or his family. He thought he was ten feet tall and bulletproof.

Nothing was more important to my daddy than a good horse show. We all loaded up and went to the horse show in Crossville almost every Saturday night. At one of the shows, Marlon was riding a little walking horse, and Daddy was looking on with much pride. One of the local police officers came up and informed Daddy that his barn was on fire. The officer was astonished that Daddy stood there and continued watching the show. Finally he realized that Daddy wasn't leaving, and he said to him again, "Mr. Kilpatrick, your barn is on fire!" Daddy calmly looked over at the young officer and said, "Can't you see I'm watching a horse show? Besides, it'll be burned down by the time I get there." When the show was over, we all went home, rescued the horses from the barn, and proceeded to put the fire out. Now, I don't know if someone deliberately set that fire or not, but, either way, it didn't really matter. Nothing took priority over the horse show. Daddy had much pride, and he liked to show off his horses. He was a distinguished, well-dressed cowboy. He always had his horse saddled and a bottle of moonshine in his saddle bag.

One of our favorite things to do as a family was to load up and take off to the rodeo in Birmingham. The rodeo was my sport. One year, when I was just a young boy, Gene Autry and Johnny Mack Brown came to town. Johnny Mack was watching me with the horses and asked my parents if he could take me to California with him to train horses. Now, I don't know if he was serious or just kidding, but my mother would absolutely not agree to it. I missed my chance at breaking and training horses for the rich and famous. Sometimes I wonder what my life would have been like if she had agreed to let me go. Imagine a small country boy like me breaking horses for a Western hero. I still think about that from time to time.

I learned to ride, rope, and break a horse by the time I was six years old. At age seven, I was buying and selling my own horses. As a young boy, I was never passionate about the idea of a formal education. My lessons were learned the hard way. My teacher was a man who demanded hard work and respect from his eldest son. He depended on me for everything, and he trained me well. Daddy taught us boys to fear no man. When I was around ten years old, I was bottling moonshine and delivering it. Late one night, my brother Billy and I had a load of shine and pockets full of money. As we approached a moonlit backwoods road, I spotted a man up in a tree. I'm sure his intention was to rob us and take our shine, but I didn't give him the chance. I shot him out of the tree, but he managed to get away. I never allowed fear to be a part of my life. A gun in my hand was as natural as a bottle in the hand of a baby, thanks to my daddy. Daddy would make us line up old cans and bottles along the fencepost. Then we would ride our horses as fast as we could and shoot the cans and bottles while riding. We got a whipping for each can we missed. Daddy did not spare the rod. Today it would be child abuse. I think it was just the time, the era in which we lived. Sometimes we accidentally shot other things. One day, my brother Billy was looking in the mirror, practicing drawing his gun. Our younger brother, Harold, came into the room and spooked him. Billy accidentally shot the gun, and the bullet ricocheted off a frying pan. Raising a bunch of rowdy boys can be a dangerous thing. There was never a dull moment and very little peace and quiet at the Kilpatrick home.

My father taught me to break high-spirited horses and mules before I could ride them. We had a couple of demon-possessed mules that were mean as the devil himself. I was plowing with those mules one day when a man stopped by the house and asked my daddy if he would sell them. Daddy repeatedly told him they were not for sale, but the man was very persistent. After several attempts to buy the mules, Daddy got tired of arguing with him and sold them. However, he warned the man. He specifically told him that they were mean and dangerous, and he doubted if he would be able to handle them. Regardless, the man said, "There is no mule that I can't handle." He was about three sheets to the wind when he made that foolish statement. Daddy took his money, and we delivered the mules. In a couple of days, the man showed up at our farm again, begging Daddy to take the mules back, because he couldn't handle them. Daddy bought the mules back at a very good price and turned a good profit. He sent me, a ten-year-old kid, to fetch those mules home. When I got there, the man had them in the barn in a stable. The man had a cotton wagon, so I told him to back the wagon out into the hall of the barn so the mules couldn't get out on either side. Then I told him to let the mules out of the stable and to stand at the back of the barn with a pitchfork; I told him that if they tried to run by him, he should poke them from behind with the pitchfork. He said,

"It will kill them if I poke them with the pitchfork." I told him that it wouldn't kill them because it was too far away from their heart. When we got them in the cotton wagon, I put bailing wire around the bottom jaw of the mules and led them off the wagon. Then I tied the mules together from head to tail. I got on my pony and was leading the mules home when I met Daddy. He was bringing the truck to see if I needed any help. Daddy went on up to the barn to talk to the man, who was just standing there in disbelief. He said to my daddy, "That just beats all I've ever seen. I'm a grown man, and I can't handle these mules, but a ten-year-old boy can." Looking back now, I don't remember being afraid of anything, even as a child. I'm not sure if that was a good thing or not. It was another trait handed down from my father, the fearless Aubrey Kilpatrick.

Daddy would buy crazy mules that nobody else would even attempt to break. The mules would be delivered to the store at Double Bridges, not far from where we lived. My brother Harold and I would ride double on a pony to the store. When we got there, we would take one of the mules out in the field beside the store and break the mule to ride home. One of us would twist the mule's ear and bite down on it while the other one was on the mule's back, ready to sit down in the saddle. When the one on the mule was ready, he would holler, "Let go!" When we let go, the ear would stand up, and then we would swing a hickory pole and hit the ears. The ears were so long they would wrap around the pole. Then, we would swing the pole again and hit the ears from the other side. The mule was in so much pain it never knew when we sat down in the saddle. The animal didn't think about bucking because its ears hurt so badly. We would kick the mule in the side a few times and run the mule around the field until it was too tired to do anything but ride. Then we would put wire around the other mule's jaw and tie the two head to tail. We would ride the pony and the mule that we broke back to the house. A lot of the old-timers would gather at the store to watch us. They couldn't believe two young boys could break wild mules. It became an event that the old-timers looked forward to. Mr. Ollie Odell would always say, "I don't think you boys will be able to break these mules." I would quickly reply, "Well, I ain't walking home." I never did walk home; instead, I rode a mule.

We had a mare that was high-spirited and crazy, and Daddy rode her with pride. He rode her into town on a Saturday afternoon, and a man approached him and asked if he could take her for a ride. The man was obviously drunk, so Daddy refused to let him ride her. The man kept pushing his buttons until Daddy finally got tired and irritated. The man jumped up on the horse, and she went crazy. The wild mare ran away with the man, and he had no control over her. He slid down to one side of the horse, hit a power pole head first, and died instantly. After that day, whenever the Kilpatrick family was out riding, people would say to their children, "Get in the house—there's Aubrey Kilpatrick with that killer horse!" There was never a horse that Daddy couldn't ride, and he rode them well and with pride.

Daddy would send me to Gadsden to round up workers for the farm. I was twelve years old, driving a big-ton farm truck with no driver's license. I was having trouble getting good help, because the man down the road was paying a nickel more an hour. Daddy had a brainstorm. He told me to fill up water bottles for the workers each day. On one particular day, he had me fill half the bottles with moonshine and the other half with water. He advised me to ask the workers if they wanted a bottle of water or a bottle of "good water." Of course they chose the "good water." Needless to say, after that day, the word got out about Aubrey Kilpatrick's "good water." We had men begging to work on our farm! They would ask me if we were the farmers with the "good water" from Sand Mountain. I would come back from Gadsden with that ton truck loaded down with men hanging on the running boards. That was a clever idea, and it worked. What man wouldn't put in an honest day's work for an honest pay and a bottle of moonshine to boot?

I respected my father, and I never said no to him. Many times he drank too much and got involved in things he had no business getting involved in. I would drive him and his friends around while they drank and had a good time. I would have rather been coon hunting or riding horses, but I was the designated driver. However, I did even the score a little. When my brother Billy and I got mad at Daddy, we would put laxatives in his moonshine. One night, a fellow from the city came out to our place, looking to buy some shine. He took a taxi out to our farm. We sold him a bottle of our best, seasoned with a little something extra. The man spent most of that night in the cornfield and didn't make it back to the city until about five hours later. The taxi driver thought the guy was dying, so he came back to check on him. The poor fellow experienced the wrath of the Kilpatrick brothers. He never bought shine from us again! Before the taxi driver pulled away, he told us we would not have to fertilize the cornfield.

The childhood memories of a young lad growing up during that era should involve swimming in the creek, hunting possums, and fishing. Times were hard, though, and all I knew was work. I don't remember being a child. I never learned to swim, but I could ride, rope, and break a horse; drive a truck; shoot a gun; and deliver a load of moonshine before I finished elementary school. I did attend school, but I was always looking for an excuse to leave. Every day I rode my pony to school, tied him (very loosely) to the tree, and went inside with a sheepish grin. Just when it was time for class to start, my pony would get loose and run away. I would explain to my teacher that I had to catch him or I would be in some serious trouble! I would have ridden my horses rather than eat when I was hungry. Riding a horse was one of my earliest memories. I felt free and in control. My teacher, Mrs. Watts, was on to me, but for some reason she liked me and extended mercy. I would ride our big goat with a wagon hitched to him and give the boys and girls a ride at school. It was a quick way to make friends. I finished the sixth grade and never made it to the seventh. There was too much work to be done, and my daddy needed me to work the farm. I don't begrudge my father for that. He did the best he could by us. I was the oldest son, and my daddy expected a lot from me.

By no means did I have a normal childhood. My father's generation was hard. His love was tough love, but I had all the things I needed. I learned many valuable lessons about life, such as work hard, respect your parents, fear no man, and don't go looking for trouble. Trouble will come looking for you, and when it does, face it head on and don't cower. I learned a lot about being a man; little did I know how much that was preparing me for the journey ahead. I was going to a place where I would need all the skills my father had taught me as a child.

My teenage years would leave a scar that would penetrate much deeper than the skin.

"Even a child is known by his doings, whether it be pure, or whether it be right." (Proverbs 20:11 KJV)

CHAPTER TWO:
THE ENEMY STRIKES

The moonshine business was thriving, and the crops looked healthy in the spring of 1951. *I Love Lucy* premiered on CBS, and *Dennis the Menace* appeared in newspapers across the United States. We didn't own a television set or a radio.

We would go over to my uncle's house to listen to the *Grand Ole Opry* on his radio. That was a highlight of Saturday night. You could buy a new car for $1,800.00, and a gallon of gas was $0.27. Harry S. Truman was president, and life expectancy was sixty-eight years old. Well, for some people it was sixty-eight; not everyone would be that fortunate.

May 17, 1951, started out as a typical day, but little did I know trouble was brewing. I was up at the crack of dawn, taking care of the horses, bottling moonshine, and plowing the fields. It seemed like any other day at the Kilpatrick farm. Daddy had been down to Florida to sell a load of meal and was scheduled to be home later that day. While he was away on business, one of the tenant farmers didn't show up to work. Instead of planting a crop of cotton, he had been laid up several days drinking and gambling. There was always a rowdy bunch hanging out over there. When Daddy got home later that day, we went over to confront the farmer. Daddy got out of the truck, knocked on the door, and asked them why they were not working in the field, planting their crops. Several of the guys came toward my daddy, threatening to whip him. Daddy pulled his gun, hit them upside the head one at a time, and stacked them all up on the porch like a pile of wood. The tenant farmer grabbed a gun, sneaked out the back door, and came around the house toward my daddy. I leaned out of the truck, stuck my gun out the window, pointed it at him, and told him if he wanted to live he better drop that gun. He threw the gun down and ran off. They'd all had too much to drink that day. They all exchanged a few words, and Daddy told a couple of the boys to get off his land and if he ever saw them again he would shoot them. Some men like to run off at the mouth when they've had too much to drink, and sometimes they fight. Such was the case that day. A fight broke out, and threats were made. Daddy was angry, and he wasn't a man who walked away from trouble. He believed in confronting things head on and dealing with them. He was willing to give the farmer one more chance to redeem himself, but that was not going to happen.

The chief of police was a good and honest man. You could take him at his word. He came out to the house and talked to Daddy about what had happened with the tenant farmer and the boys. He told Daddy that a warrant may be sworn out for his arrest. Daddy told the chief he would be in the next morning if a warrant was sworn out for him. It was getting late, and everyone was tired. The chief of police told Daddy he should just burn the house down and get those tenant farmers off his land. Daddy should have listened to him. They'd caused trouble for the last farmer they'd worked for also. Daddy thought that was the end of it, but evil had reared its ugly head, and the enemy was about to attack. A couple of the sheriff's deputies had received a call about the incident. They drove out to the farm and talked to me for a while. They asked me what had happened, and I told them. They never did go down to the house and talk to Daddy. I explained the situation to them, and they drove off. When the sheriff got word, he went out to the tenant farmers' house and pressed the boys to swear out a warrant for my daddy. The charge was assault with intent to murder. The sheriff hated Daddy, and the feeling was mutual. Some folks around here say the sheriff was afraid of Aubrey Kilpatrick and he wanted him dead. The sheriff showed up at the chief of police's house later that night. The chief explained to him that he had talked to Aubrey Kilpatrick and that the situation was under control. Tempers flared, words were exchanged, and threats were made. The sheriff threatened the chief, and he was forced to go, against his will, with the sheriff and his deputies to the Kilpatrick farm that night. The chief of police didn't have a choice in the matter, according to his wife.

My brother Billy and Fred Howard had been out possum hunting. The two boys were minding their own business when the sheriff, his deputies, and the chief of police pulled up. The sheriff asked the boys who they were and why they were out so late. Billy told him he was Aubrey Kilpatrick's boy and that they had been possum hunting. The sheriff told them to get in the car. Billy wouldn't leave the dog, so they put the dog in the trunk of the car. They made Billy ride up front, and they put Fred Howard in the backseat. There were six people in the car and a dog in the trunk.

Daddy had just sat down and taken his boots off, and Mother was finishing up some last-minute chores before turning in for the night. I had been out at the barn to check on the horses. Someone had tried to burn one of our barns down the night before. I was standing in the kitchen, getting a drink of water, when I heard a commotion. It was around 11:45 p.m. when the law pulled up at our place. They were in an unmarked car. Daddy pulled on his boots and opened the front door of the old farmhouse. As he stepped outside, one of the deputies rolled down the little side window of the car and shot Daddy twice. Daddy pulled his gun and fired back in self-defense as he fell to the ground. Billy and Fred Howard watched as our daddy died. As I came out the back door and around the house, I felt the heat from bullets flying by my head. They were shooting at me, too. I didn't know it was the law. It was so dark I couldn't see anything. I caught a glimpse of my daddy lying in a puddle of blood. I felt like everything was moving in slow motion. I went back in the house, grabbed a carbine, and came out of the house. Just as I walked out of the house, Fred Howard broke loose and ran by me. I can't believe I didn't shoot that kid. I had no idea that one of the deputies was holding Billy, my brother, in front of him as a shield. He couldn't pull away, and he was forced to watch as they tried to kill me, too. Then I shot the deputy in the head as my brother broke free and hid behind the well. Thankfully the bullet missed Billy. I kept shooting until the shooting stopped. About that time, my brother Harold ran by me into the back door. He was spending the night next door at Fred Gobles's place. When they heard all the shooting, they came to see what was going on. One of the deputies was holding a rag over his neck where I had shot him. When he saw Harold run into the yard, he reached for his gun. There was a brief moment of silence. I got down on my belly and crawled around to the other side of the house. Then one of them yelled, "Hey, Kilpatrick, everybody is down but me. How about letting me go?" It was one of the sheriff's deputies. I told him to throw out his gun, and I would let him go. He crawled to the car and drove away. Another deputy was wounded and managed to crawl into the car with him as he was driving away. One of the deputies died, and the other one lived. I was surprised that Billy, Fred, and Harold were still alive. I didn't have time to be afraid. I was just trying to save my family. I had no idea if Mother and the other children were unharmed.

The chief of police was dead too. He'd jumped out of the car and run toward the house, but he'd been shot in the back, possibly by one of his own. There is no way Daddy or I could have shot him in the back. The chief had never drawn his gun from his holster. I will always believe he was trying to get to me and my family to help us. I regret that man lost his life. It saddened me deeply. He had always been good to me and my family. He did not deserve to die, and I believe he laid his life down to help the Kilpatrick family that night. They wouldn't allow an autopsy on his body. Some things will always remain a mystery.

When the dust settled, the chief of police, the sheriff, a sheriff's deputy, and my daddy, Aubrey Kilpatrick, were all dead. Mother and the children were safe and unharmed. Mother was four months pregnant with another son. I could now hear the cries and the mourning. I had stood brave to protect them. I wasn't afraid, and I didn't cower. Daddy would have been proud of me. My biggest regret was that I couldn't save him. If I had it to do over, I would. The man, the father I loved and respected, was gone, shot down in cold-blooded murder. He looked so broken and frail lying there. That picture haunts me to this day. He was young, ambitious, full of life, and thirty-nine years old. What a waste.

It was a horrible tragedy. I have often wondered, what if the situation had been handled differently? For instance, what if the sheriff had gotten out of the car and knocked on the front door? What if the sheriff had asked Daddy to come peacefully down to the station? But most of all, I ask myself, what if the sheriff had listened to the chief of police? This senseless act and all the bloodshed could have been prevented. Why would they pick my brothers up and put them in harm's way? Why would they shoot into a house where children were sleeping? Why would they shoot at a sixteen-year-old boy trying to save his family? Why not allow Aubrey Kilpatrick to turn himself in the next day? There is a right way and a wrong way to handle every situation. This was handled wrong, and the outcome was devastating not only for my family but for the families of all those who lost their lives that night.

Wives lost husbands, children lost their fathers, mothers lost their sons, and I lost my youth and innocence. An entire county mourned the devastation of that night. That picture is still as clear as the day it happened, and the hurt remains. I desperately wish things had turned out differently. We can't go back, so we must go forward. Where was the justice in all this? I searched for that answer my entire life.

Many newspaper articles have been written about that night, but not one of them told my side of the story. No newspaper interviewed me or my family about what we witnessed that night. No reporter asked my family what they saw and heard. It was reported as being an ambush, something spectacular. It was neither of those things. It was a horrifying tragedy. Some say it was the bloodiest gunfight in northeast Alabama history. I know what it was—I was there. It was wrong. Everything about that dreadful night was wrong. It should have never happened.

I was angry, outraged, and in shock. I felt something warm running down my face. I thought it was blood, but as I wiped my face, I realized it was tears. I was crying.

"No weapon that is formed against thee shall prosper." (Isaiah 54:17 KJV)

CHAPTER THREE: INNOCENCE LOST

Within minutes, the local police and sheriff's department were swarming the place. Law enforcement officers from neighboring counties were also there. I can't explain all the emotions that were racing through my mind. The officials were very disrespectful to my family that night, especially Mother. One of the officers threatened and cursed her. Mother was hysterical because she had just witnessed her husband's murder. Her entire family had been put in harm's way; she had every right to be emotional. My little brother Russell was sitting in Mother's lap, crying, and all the children were terrified. They had never witnessed such a horrible tragedy in their young lives. The law was frantically searching for answers and trying to get to the truth of the matter, but they had no right treating my family the way they did. The law enforcement officers thought we were responsible for the tragic event. They claimed it was an ambush and that Daddy had all us boys staked out, armed and dangerous, waiting to gun down the law. That was not the truth at all. What happened on May 17 was traumatizing, and we were all in shock. I thought after talking to Daddy and the law that day that everything was under control. I was wrong, dead wrong.

The law questioned me, and I tried to explain what had happened. It had all happened so fast that it was hard to give a lot of details. I was arrested and taken to the Etowah County jail by a man named Bradford. Mr. Bradford was a family man with children of his own and a son who was my age. He talked to me in a calm voice and treated me like a human being. He had a gentle spirit about him.

I did not know until later that Billy and Harold and two of our tenant farmers, Fred and Tom, had also been arrested. It was Harold's fourteenth birthday, one he would never forget. I was outraged when

I found out my little brothers had been arrested and had to spend the night in jail. Tom and Fred had no part in the shooting, and they had no idea what had happened. Tom lived a quarter of a mile down the road. He was in bed asleep when it happened. One of the neighbors woke him up to tell him what had taken place down at our farm. Tom pulled on his overalls, no shirt, no shoes, and that is what he was wearing when he was arrested.

The law was grasping at straws and accusing everybody in sight. They were in a panic, and I totally understood that. We were all taken to the Etowah County jail in separate cars. They searched us and handcuffed us when we arrived. Billy and Harold, after being questioned, were released the next day. I will never know what that did to them and how traumatizing it was. They were children, and even though I was only sixteen years old, I had been a man my entire life. For some unknown reason, I had no fear about where I was and where I was going. On Sunday night, they transferred Tom, Fred, and me to the Marshall County jail in separate cars. They put me in a car with four men. Mr. Bradford was one of the men, and he actually stayed with me for several days. I wasn't afraid, but he was concerned that someone would try to kill me. The Marshall County jail was in an uproar. They put all three of us in the same cell to see if we would talk. Tom and Fred didn't have a clue what happened the night of May 17. Fred served ninety-six days in the county jail, and Tom served ninety days. They were innocent bystanders who were taken from their families and robbed of income for three months. Times were hard enough for tenant farmers without being falsely accused of murder and thrown in jail. It was unnecessary and made no sense at all.

I longed to be with my family. Aubrey Kilpatrick was dead, and his widow, Elizabeth, was left to raise eight children from ages sixteen months to sixteen years old. The child she was carrying in her womb would be born dead on September 2, 1951. I was now the man of the house, but I would not be able to fulfill that role, so a lot of responsibility fell to my brothers Billy and Harold. Mother would bury her dead and send her oldest son off to jail. Elizabeth Kilpatrick had the weight of the world on her shoulders. How would she care for and feed all those hungry children? My little sister, Faye, was deaf from birth and only three years old at the time of the shooting. The baby, Danny, was sixteen months old. They would never know or remember their daddy. I worried about them all the time, but I would never know the grief and anxiety that Mother was dealing with.

I was not allowed to attend my daddy's funeral, even though my mother needed me there to help her through that day. I was very thankful that Billy and Harold were able to go. I had no closure, and it would be years before the healing would penetrate into my heart and soul. I mourned for my father, the fearless Aubrey Kilpatrick. I honor his memory to this day.

Six days after the shooting, the chief of police's widow and her children came to visit Mother. She told Mother the events leading up to the night of the shooting and how her husband had been threatened. They talked about how hard their lives would be for them and their children. The two women mourned for their husbands. Before the shooting, they'd lived very different lives, but now they had so much in common. They were widows left to raise their children alone because of one unnecessary act that shattered many lives forever.

I spent one year and one day in the county jail. I celebrated my seventeenth birthday locked behind bars. I was given one meal a day with small portions and about a half glass of hot tap water. I craved Mother's biscuits and gravy. They tried to starve me to death, but I refused to die. They hated me because I was Aubrey Kilpatrick's boy, bad blood. Now I was reaping what he had sown. They were out for revenge because I was responsible for killing three of their officers. They continued questioning me over and over. I was allowed no activity at all, so I just sat and looked at the four walls day and night. They would leave the door open in hopes that I would try to escape so they could shoot me, but my father had not raised a fool. Sometimes at night I could picture myself escaping, but I knew there would be more grief to bear. It was summertime and extremely hot. I would wet a towel in the toilet bowl and lie on it to cool off, because I didn't have a shirt. They turned the cold water off in my cell, so all I had was hot water to drink. They thought they would break my spirit like they'd break a horse, but they didn't. I felt like a slave in bondage, and I longed for freedom. I could close my eyes and envision myself riding my horse into the wind. Nothing is better than freedom—you realize that when it is taken away. If it hadn't been for Jessie Camp, I would have starved to death and died in that place. But I wouldn't give them the satisfaction. Mr. Camp was sworn in as sheriff in Marshall County a few months after my arrest. He came into the jail to visit me, and he was outraged at my condition. I weighed 120 pounds when I was arrested, and I weighed 73 pounds when he came to visit me. I was so weak I could barely walk. Mr. Camp made sure I received appropriate clothing, food, and a haircut. Jessie Camp was a good man who showed me mercy.

The days and nights all ran together. I missed my family, my horses, and my freedom. I had always thought my life was hard and that I had missed out on a lot of things. At this moment in my life, I would have given anything to be back on the farm, hauling moonshine, plowing fields, and breaking wild horses. I had no idea what was going to happen from one day to the next. I relived May 17, 1951, every day of my life. I played it over and over in my mind, trying to make sense of it and sort it out. It haunted me.

Mother hired a couple of good lawyers, George Rogers and John Brown. She spent over $27,000.00 trying to prove my innocence. She never gave up on me, and she fought the county with every fiber of her being. It was physically and mentally exhausting for the entire family. We knew the truth—it was self-defense—but we would never be able to prove it. We were not responsible for all that bloodshed. Our lawyers wanted to subpoena the chief of police's widow, but Mother would not allow it. She had suffered deeply, and calling her to testify would only prolong her healing and put her in harm's way.

Mother had never worked outside the home or away from the farm.

She had worked beside her husband, tending to the farm, the home, and the children. Now she was spending what money she had trying to keep me out of prison. Mother took a job at the poultry plant in Albertville. She never took the time to learn to drive, so she walked to work and back each day. It would be dark when she walked home at night. When a car would come by, she would run and hide in the cornfield, because she was afraid. Most people were kind and friendly to her, but others were not. After all, she was Aubrey Kilpatrick's widow, and she was constantly in danger. Some people were cruel, and they made false accusations. In the fall of 1951, my brother Harold had to have emergency surgery to remove his appendix. He was only fourteen years old and a very sick boy. My oldest sister, Jeretta, became the caregiver for the children at the tender age of twelve. She was still a child herself and was forced to grow up quickly. Her youth was stripped away. Life as we knew it would never be the same. My entire family suffered from the loss of Daddy. Mother's burdens were heavy, and the weight of the world was on her shoulders.

We were not the only family suffering. I thought about the wives and children of the other men who lost their lives that night. This event would remain fresh in the minds of many for years to come. Anger, guilt, and bitterness can destroy a person's life. Would any of us ever be able to recover from this horrible tragedy?

I was beginning to lose hope until I received a letter from a young lady named Ann Scott. My mother met her after one of the trials, and she asked her to write to me while I was in jail. We started writing, and then she came to visit me one Sunday. We could talk to each other through a small opening in the door. I was shy and awkward and looked like death. I was glad all she could see was my eyes. All my insecurities vanished when I looked into her blue eyes. She was the most beautiful creature I had ever seen. You could say it was love at first sight or divine intervention. Ann sparked a ray of hope in my messed-up life and gave me a reason to live. Thoughts of her consumed me and made life worth living.

Mother visited me every chance she could. On one visit, she asked the guard if he would open the door just long enough for her to hug me. Surprisingly enough, he did, and she sobbed uncontrollably. I tried to be strong for her and hold back my tears. At this crucial time in her life, when she needed me the most, I was helpless. I was very thankful Ann was with her that day. That was the first time I was able to see the lady with the beautiful blue eyes. Ann Scott took my breath away.

It is a good thing to have a sense of humor. Laughter can keep a person from going crazy. I was having stomach problems, because I was not allowed to eat but one small portion of food per day while I was in the county jail. Mother brought me some Carter's Liver Pills to help with the stomach problems I was having. The town drunk (we'll call him Ken) got arrested for public intoxication about once a week. He called me Little Buddy Kilpatrick. Ken knew my daddy and everything that happened on May 17. He always got put in the cell next to me, and he was very annoying. One night, they brought him in as I was taking one of the pills. Old Ken asked me what I was putting in my mouth, and I told him it was a nerve pill. He asked if he could have one, because he had the shakes (he was sobering up). An hour passed, and he asked if he could have another one, because the first one didn't seem to be working. I politely obliged. He took about four pills in a few hours, and then the pills started to work. Ken thought it was the liquor working out of his system, and I never told him the truth. I laughed all night. He didn't annoy me that night, but I sure annoyed him! It felt good to laugh, even if it was at the expense of another.

After one year and one day of being caged like an animal, I was released on bond for eighteen months. It was May 18, 1952, and Dures Thomas and Sam Bruce posted my bond. They were friends with my daddy, and they extended help to my family. It felt so good walking out of jail into the sunshine and breathing the fresh Sand Mountain air. I could not believe my eyes when we pulled up at the homestead. People were everywhere. Hundreds had come out to welcome me home and show their support. I had never felt so loved and had never had so many hugs. It was wonderful to be reunited with my family. The whole community turned out, and we had good food and good fellowship. Home had never looked better. As happy as I was to be out and be reunited with my family, there was sadness in my heart, because Daddy wasn't there. It was tormenting to walk around the house and remember the events that had taken place there on May 17, 1951. I missed Daddy. I had always felt his presence in my life and in our home, but now there was a void in our lives that no one could ever fill.

My next stop was the home of Ann Scott. I couldn't wait to see her again and meet her parents, Orb and Tiny Scott. They treated me very respectfully. I wasn't sure how they would react to their only child dating a convict headed to prison. They treated me like a son and never questioned me about what had actually happened on May 17. Ann made me feel special. We sat on the front porch swing and talked. I asked her parents if she could go to visit my family, and they agreed. I was surprised that they allowed her to go. I felt peace when I was with her. Being with her felt like home to me. This was a place where I felt I belonged, a place I would come to love. Ann believed in me.

I was free, once again. This was the best day of my life.

"A light shined in the prison and his chains fell off . . ." (*Acts 12:7 KJV*)

CHAPTER FOUR:
RAY OF HOPE

The long, lazy days of summer and Ann Scott by my side—what more could a guy ask for? We started a beautiful courtship, and I had a glimmer of hope for a better life. I took her out to eat and to the Shady Side drive-in or the Rialto Theater almost every weekend. We had been out on several dates before I ever got up the nerve to kiss her. Then one night I was lost in her blue eyes, and I politely asked her if I could have a kiss. The answer was yes, and I wanted it to last forever. I lost my heart to her that night.

I would eat supper at Ann's house often, especially on Sunday. I would always slip a five-dollar bill under my plate to show my appreciation to her mother. She would fuss at me for doing it, but I insisted that she keep it. Tiny Scott was a wonderful cook, and she could make some of the finest apple pies. I loved her like a mother, and she treated me like a son. Tiny was from a large family of twelve children. They were a close-knit family, and they showed me much love and support. I felt like Ann's daddy, Orb, was one of my best friends. We would have many long conversations sitting on his front porch. He was an easy man to talk to, and it was easy to open up to him. Ann's family became an important part of my life. I wanted these days to last forever, but I knew they were slipping by too fast.

When I was released from the Guntersville jail, my uncle, C. W. Cofield, gave me a job driving cars to the sale. "Hot Dang" Otinger also hauled cars. He once bought a monkey at an auction. We were hauling a load of cars back from the sale, and Hot Dang brought the monkey with us. We stopped by a bar on the way back, and he took the monkey into the bar, poured beer into an ashtray, and let the monkey drink it.

When we left the bar, Hot Dang was driving, and the monkey was in the car with him. The monkey was hugging and loving on him, and Hot Dang was getting mad, so he put him in the backseat of the car he was towing behind him. In those days, you hooked cars together bumper to bumper to haul them. The monkey passed out and slept for a while, but then he woke up, hopped up in the front seat of the car, and started turning the steering wheel back and forth like he was driving. He was mimicking us! The car got loose and ended up in the field, wrecked. We had to stop at a gas station, and, for some unknown reason, Hot Dang took the monkey in the store. The monkey went crazy and trashed the place. Hot Dang took him back to the auction, and they sold him to someone else. It wasn't long until the monkey returned to the auction for the third time. This time the auctioneer said, "All sales final. You buy the monkey, you keep the monkey!" Lesson learned. Never give beer to a monkey, and never let a monkey drive.

Love, laughter, and family had now taken the place of doom, gloom, and loneliness. This would be a summer I would cherish for many years to come. I would hold these memories close to my heart, and they would see me through some very dark days ahead. I was working, making money, and courting Ann Scott. Hope had been restored.

Family and friends started a petition to keep me out of prison. Hundreds of people signed it statewide. More people signed that petition than any other petition ever signed in the state of Alabama. We had a lot of support from so many people. The Kilpatrick family needed that, and we were grateful.

One night, while I was visiting Ann, Mother saw a strange man snooping around our place. She was so frightened for their safety that she took a gun and sneaked out the back door. Mother shot toward the man, and he ran off into the woods. The following morning, we found bloodstains on the ground. My mother would always live in fear that someone was out to hurt her and the children. I feared for my family all the time, and soon I would be leaving them, again. Life was unfair and cruel at times.

The trials were long and trying. My brother Billy had to testify at all the trials but was not allowed to stay in the courtroom during the hearings. The first trial, in the fall of 1951, was for the murder of the sheriff. I had fifteen character witnesses, of which two were ministers. Marlon Smith's mother, Ms. Effie, was one of the character witnesses. Judge Stone asked the jury to take into consideration that I was a well mannered and hardworking boy. I was sentenced to seventeen years. In April of 1952, the Alabama Court of Appeals reversed the decision on a technical error. After that, there were two trials that ended in a mistrial. In total, there were five trials in twenty-two months. The murder charges against me for the shooting of the sheriff were dropped. I was charged with manslaughter in the shooting of the chief of police, and that was also dropped. Then I was charged with assault with intent to murder the sheriff's deputy, and those charges were dropped. The last trial was for first-degree manslaughter for the killing of the deputy sheriff.

The toxicologist for the Birmingham division of the Department of Public Safety testified that in regards to the three shots fired through the window of the car, the two fired from inside the car going out were fired before the one shot came into the car from the outside. Who knows—if we had not exhausted our resources, and if I had been strong enough to continue the grueling trials, maybe, just maybe, justice would have eventually prevailed. But I didn't have any fight left in me. Mother was exhausted, and everything had taken a toll on her. I could see it in her eyes.

The state first held out for a twenty-year term for all charges but reduced it to fifteen years, then twelve, and finally ten. My lawyer, Mr. Rogers, appealed the case immediately. He said, "I believe we can win." But he also knew we had exhausted our finances and that in the end we might not win. We talked about voluntary surrender. He said I would make trustee automatically and that it would be easier on me in the end. After a brief moment, I agreed to accept the terms offered by the state. No matter what really happened that night, and no matter how hard we tried to prove my innocence, I knew in my heart I was fighting a losing battle. Strangely enough, when I agreed to a voluntary surrender on November 18, 1953, I felt the weight of the world lift off my shoulders. It had been a long, drawn-out battle, and my family was exhausted, physically, mentally, and financially. I felt relief until I heard Ann crying out loud. Mixed emotions flooded my heart and mind.

The judge gave me a few weeks to get things in order before I had to report to Kilby Prison to start my ten-year sentence. How do you say goodbye to those you love? How do you turn and walk away from a mother who needs you so desperately? How do you let go? Looking into the eyes of my little sisters and brothers, I could see sadness and despair. I couldn't help but wonder who would take care of them and how they'd survive without Daddy. Mother was so worried about me, and she was afraid prison would change who I was on the inside. I had no idea what I was about to face, but I knew it would be the hardest thing I would ever have to do.

I sat on the front porch swing at Ann's house with her by my side. I wanted to ask her to wait for me, but I knew it would be unfair. I had no idea where my future was headed or if I would even have a future. Was I destined to spend the rest of my life behind bars? Would I ever see her face again? Ann's mom called her in at midnight. Sadness and despair filled my heart as I kissed her goodbye and embraced her that night. It was all I could do to hold back my tears; it was tearing me apart. As I looked in her eyes, tears began to roll off her cheeks, and I felt hope slipping away. If I had any fear at all, it was the fear of losing her to someone else.

"For God has not given us the spirit of fear; but of power, and of love, and of a sound mind." (2 Timothy 1:7 KJV)

CHAPTER FIVE:
CHAINS OF BONDAGE/
DAYS AT DRAPER

In December of 1953, I reported to Kilby correctional facility in Montgomery, Alabama. I would not be able to stay and serve my time there because of my age. Unfortunately, I would be sent to Draper Prison to serve my time in maximum security with grown men. That did not come as a surprise to me, because I had always been expected to act like an adult, even as a young boy. The warden at Kilby correctional facility was good to me while I was there, and he allowed me to drive the inmates to the doctor and the dentist. He showed me compassion. + Life would have been much easier for me at Kilby but I was on my way to Draper.

I was transferred to Draper Prison in Elmore, Alabama, on December 15, 1953. I was welcomed by Warden Reeves. The warden was about six feet tall and three hundred pounds; he wore glasses and smoked a cigar. I was a short, skinny boy, and we looked like David and Goliath. Warden Reeves looked over his wire-rimmed glasses and said, "I didn't send for you, and I can't do anything about it, so you better not mess up, or I'll send you to lock-up."

Lock-up was a small cubbyhole with a table and a commode poured in concrete. It was so small you couldn't stand up, so your back and legs hurt constantly because of poor circulation. They stripped you down as naked as the day you were born and put you in this small space. Around 9:30 at night, they would take you to a small cell to sleep. The only things in the cell were a cot and a bucket. You would hold your arms up over your head, and they would lower a bag that looked like

29

a pillowcase down on a rope from the ceiling. That was your gown to sleep in. You never got the same "gown," and I don't think they ever washed them. They were different lengths, some short and some long. The guards would wake you up at 3:30 a.m. and transfer you back to lock-up. It was bitter cold in the winter.

The day I arrived at Draper, I went to the bathroom to find that one of the inmates had been killed in there just minutes before. No one had cleaned the mess up, and his brains were still splattered all over the walls. I'd always considered myself a tough boy, but now I wasn't sure. Draper Prison was not the county jail, and nothing could have prepared me for that scene.

There were no assigned cells or beds at Draper. You had to find your own, and you had to pay for it. I was given one set of clothes and one pair of shoes. I wore a 25 waist in pants, and they gave me a size 36. The shoes they gave me were a size 10, and I wore a size 5. Daddy had a couple of friends at Draper, Clayton Williams and Fred Wells, and, fortunately, they had a cell, bed, clothes, and shoes waiting for me when I got there. They made sure my needs were met, and they looked out for me. I sure was glad they were there. It didn't take me long to realize that I needed a job and an income. You had to buy everything in prison.

The men quickly named me "Little Man," and it stuck. I was given a job in the laundry room. If you were offered a job, you'd better not turn it down. Those who refused to work were sent to the "doghouse." Lock-up was bad, but the doghouse was worse. First, they would tie you to a fence and whip you with chains. The doghouse was a four-by-four box with only a five-gallon bucket for relieving yourself. You were given bread and water once a day. The doctor came around once a week to check on you, to make sure you were still alive. You had to serve twenty-one days in the doghouse. That was a place I never wanted to visit. I promised myself that I would work hard, make money, and mind my own business. Like Daddy said, "Don't go looking for trouble; trouble will come looking for you, and, when it does, don't cower."

When the men brought their clothes to the laundry room, they had to pay to have them steamed. If they refused to pay, we would slit the seams of their pants with a razor blade and then steam them. When they put the pants on, it looked like they were wearing a hula skirt. It was entertaining, and the other inmates would get a good laugh out of it. I had been working in laundry for over two years when I got my hand cut badly. The warden asked me if I wanted to work in the prison store. I told him I didn't want to work the store. His reply was, "You wouldn't refuse to work, would you?" I quickly answered, "No, sir." He asked why I didn't want to work the store. I told him that at about five o'clock every morning, several hundred hungry inmates would be cussing me, wanting their coffee and egg sandwiches. The warden had a solution for that. He handed me a billy club and told me to use it. So I went to work in the prison store.

One guy was always trying to steal cigarettes from the store. I was fed up with him, and I told the guard about it. The guard told me to use the billy club on him; that would take care of the problem. Sure enough, a few days later, the man came in, took a pack of cigarettes, and proceeded to run. I grabbed the billy club and went after him. He was running down the hall toward the guard's office when I hit him hard. He hit the door of the office and slid into the office and under the guard's desk. I looked at the guard and said, "You can have him." That put a stop to the cigarette thief. I got the bluff on him, and things ran smoothly after that. I tried to get the warden to take inventory of the store from time to time, but he never did, because I was honest and he trusted me. I was making many friends in prison.

I had to have dental work done when I got to Draper, because my teeth had decayed so badly. The wardens randomly chose inmates to work in the dentist's office. They were all really good to me. They always gave me shots to deaden the gums and allowed my mouth to numb before pulling my teeth. On one occasion, I had a nerve pressing on the root of a tooth. The dentist said he would need to transfer me over to Kilby to have the work done. I was in so much pain that I told him to just pull it there and be done with it. It took three men to hold me down while the doc pulled the tooth. When new inmates came in to see the dentist, I would go back first and scream and carry on like I was dying; then we would take a capsule that was the color of blood, break it open, and smear the powder from the capsule on my face. It looked like blood running off my face. You should have seen the look on some of the new inmates' faces when I walked out holding my mouth, fake blood running down my face! They would be shaking in their shoes when it was their time in the chair. You had to laugh even if it was at the expense of someone else. It made the time pass.

We could play cards and gamble all we wanted, but no dice were allowed. Every time men played dice, someone got killed. You could make lots of money playing cards, but you'd better not get caught cheating, or they would kill you. I perfected the game of Rook. One of the guys I partnered with in Rook used hand signals to cheat. Each finger represented a color. Everyone knew we were cheating, but they couldn't catch us, and they couldn't prove it. I made lots of money playing cards. Many of the gamblers from Phoenix City had been busted and sent to Draper. They had connections on the outside, and there was always a steady flow of money. Once in a while, you would find a bag stuffed full of cash stashed in a hiding place.

One of the most disgusting things I ever witnessed in Draper was when a kitten came in the kitchen and was wandering around. The inmate who was working the kitchen was cooking stew. He caught the kitten and threw it into a pot of boiling water. Then he added potatoes and onions along with eyeballs, guts, and hair. Granny Clampett from *The Beverly Hillbillies* didn't have a thing on this guy. I learned to just make the best of a bad situation. Like it or not, this was now my dwelling place and a way of life.

It was a bad idea to break line in the chow hall. The men were serious about their chow. It didn't take much for tempers to flare. Inmates were always picking a fight. I think that was one way of letting out their frustration. One day, a cocky fellow jumped ahead of several inmates, and out of nowhere this older man grabbed him by the seat of the britches and spanked him so hard he had to have stitches in his backside. I observed and learned many valuable lessons, including look straight ahead and keep your mouth shut.

The guards would take us to the field to plant crops, usually onions. The onion bulbs were in the back of a wagon that was pulled by a team of horses. Late one evening, a bad storm blew in, and the lightning ran from the sky to the ground. The older men who were serving life sentences would curse at God. They would say, "Come on, Jesus Christ, take us out of here." They were very disrespectful to God. As the words were leaving their mouths one day, lightning struck one of the horses and killed it instantly. That stirred something down deep in my being. I believed there was a God, even though I did not have a relationship with him. If you refused to work in the fields, the guards would tie you in between the mules, and you became a work mule for the day. You took every step the mules took, and you were given water when they were given water. If you drank water, you had to drink it from the trough with the mules. The next day, you couldn't wait to work in the field! Some lessons are learned the hard way.

Guys would do anything for a high in prison. They would buy nasal spray for twenty-nine cents. Then they would cut it open, take out the paraffin, and put it in their coffee. It was like a hit of speed, and they would stay up for days, playing cards. Sometimes they would take paregoric—they would boil it and snort it. Other times, they put it in a tin cup and held it over a fire. They would boil it, suck it out in a needle, and shoot it. It felt like fire going through your body, and it would take three men to hold you down. That was a crazy high, and the men would get mean and rowdy. Mint julep was another favorite in prison. Some of the recipes prisoners came up with were amazing, but where there was a will, there was a way. Whoever was working kitchen duty would steal yeast and sugar. They would walk out of the kitchen with it stuck under their arms. They would mix it up in rubber boots and sit it over the big coolers. Sometimes they would mix it in a commode, take turns sitting on it, and then drink it out of a straw. If a guard came, they would flush it. Desperate people do desperate things, but that was despicable. The only bad habit I picked up in prison was chewing on a cigar and cussing once in a while. I never had the desire to do drugs or drink. It wouldn't take away your troubles; it just numbed you for a little while, and then you had to face reality. It was easier for me to face each day head-on and sober.

The "dog warden" would randomly pick an inmate to help train the dogs. He would pick a man, take him to the field, turn him loose, and then, almost immediately, turn the dogs loose. That poor fellow would run like the wind to keep the dogs from catching him. One of the prisoners could outrun the dogs. He would show up at the gate the next day and turn himself in. Times sure have changed. In those days, you paid for your crimes. They worked you like slaves and beat you like a yard dog.

A lot of the older prisoners who were there for life would take the younger prisoners as their slaves. They would do favors in return for money and protection. You were not given the option to choose. If they chose you, then you would belong to them. Some of the young men had a chance at parole, but they would always end up back in prison. They were marked for life. I can't explain what that does to a person. Those young men were abused physically and mentally over and over, and that scarred them for life.

Once a year, the women from Tutwiler Prison would come over to Draper and put on a play. We would work day and night spit shining the place to get ready for it. You had to pay to get a front-row seat. When the women walked in, the men would go crazy, yelling and hanging off the rafters. It was always comical and something we all anticipated with excitement.

The guards all liked me and treated me well. I used to cut their hair, and I was really good at it. Back home, I used to cut my entire family's hair. One Sunday, a guard took me home with him to eat dinner, but, before we sat down to eat, the warden sent another guard to fetch me back. That was not allowed, because I was not a trustee, and I would never make trustee. One of the members of the Classification Board did not like me. He'd been friends with one of the officers I killed. I made lots of friends at Draper; even the warden became my friend. There was one guard who mistreated me and wished me dead. I would have killed him, but another guard took me aside and encouraged me. He said, "James, you don't want to spend the rest of your life in prison because of that man." I am very glad I listened to him. I was reminded that I had someone back at home waiting for me—her name was Ann Scott.

One of my best friends in prison was nicknamed "Shot-gun." His wife was terminally ill, and her medication was very expensive. Shot-gun robbed a loan company to pay for his wife's medication, and a man got killed in the process. Shot-gun was an intelligent man who found himself in a desperate situation. None of us know what we would do until we have walked in another man's shoes. Under the circumstances, I might have done the same thing. Some people would never understand why a young boy like myself would attempt a shootout with the law. If your family was put in harm's way, your first thought would be to protect the ones you loved, no matter the cost. Shot-gun was a good man, and we became good friends.

My family could visit me on the weekends. I looked forward to the visits, but I could see how hard it was on them to see me in that place. I had lots of visitors, family, friends, and neighbors, but the one I longed to see the most was Ann. When I saw her, my heart would fill with hope, and I had a vision of a future with her. I drew strength from her. Ann bought me a watch while I was there. She was faithful about visiting me and sending letters. I was strengthened and encouraged each time she came. Turning and walking away was always the hardest thing to do.

Mother got really sick twice while I was in prison. To my surprise, I was allowed to go home to visit her. The first time, it was for a couple of hours. They were going to handcuff me, but I refused to go handcuffed. I did not want Mother to see me like that, so they agreed to no handcuffs. Mother had developed heart disease, and she was a diabetic. The second time, I was allowed to stay longer, but that only made it harder to go back. I think I was good medicine for her, because she recovered quickly both times. She would always slip a little money into my hand.

After four years of living and working in this place, I was about to have a chance at freedom. I was coming up for parole, and I was going to make it. The next day started out as any other day: get up at dawn and get busy. I had forgotten about the money Mother gave me when I went to visit her. It was still in my shirt pocket, and we were not allowed to keep cash on us in prison. There was some trouble in my cell block that day, and we had a shakedown. The guard found the dollar in my pocket, and he sent me to lock-up. It was a slap in the face. No one in the state of Alabama had ever been paroled while in lock-up. That was the last thing I needed. The chance of being released looked grim. It was December and freezing cold. Adams was one of the guards and a good man. He sent me to the doctor to get penicillin shots so I wouldn't catch pneumonia and die in lock-up. I was transferred to Kilby for lock-up. When I saw Warden Deeds, he asked me what I was doing there. I told him what happened, and he said, "You're tough, ain't you? Let it go; you're going home soon." I held on to that thought. They stripped me down to nothing, not one piece of clothing, and put me in this small space. I was so cold I couldn't feel my feet and legs. The space was so small I couldn't stand up, so all I could do was sit and think. I was cold, hungry, and alone, but I could not allow that to take hold of my mind. I held on to thoughts of Ann and my family back home. Memories flooded my mind. I tried to stay focused on positive things. I refused to let them break my spirit. To my surprise, after eleven days in lock-up, I stumbled out, got a bath, shaved, and cut my hair. I received a good review from the board, and I walked out of Draper Prison on parole on December 16, 1957. After four years, I was free. That was a first for the state of Alabama. No man had ever walked out of lock-up on parole. I was given a blue suit, and all my belongings were placed in a small suitcase. As I walked out, I remembered May 17 and how hard the last six years had been. I vowed to never return to this place. I had no idea what my future held, but as I walked out of Draper Prison a free man on December 16, 1957, I could see Mother; close behind her was Ann Scott. Once again my hope was restored, and I had a glimpse of my future.

"For I know the thoughts that I think toward you, saith the Lord, thoughts of peace, and not of evil, to give you an expected end." (Jeremiah 29:11 KJV)

Childhood Days

Elizabeth Kilpatrick

Aubrey Kilpatrick

James in prison

James and the coon dogs

Ann & James wedding day

James with Orb & Tiny Scott

James riding horses with Marty, Tiger & Patrick

50th wedding anniversay

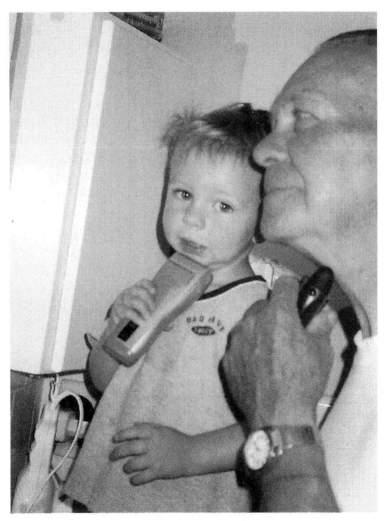

James teaching Justin to shave

CHAPTER SIX: PRESSING FORWARD

THE YEARS I SPENT in prison were wasted years, precious days gone forever, a youth I could never recapture. My thoughts were consumed with the memory of May 17. Each day was a battle to put it behind me and press forward into my future. Life in prison was hard, and it had taken a toll on me and the entire family.

I was out on parole and was prohibited from many of my rights as a citizen, such as voting. I couldn't borrow money, and I couldn't get married without permission. I had to prove myself before those privileges could be reinstated, and it would take fifteen years for that day to come.

Since the death of my daddy, Mother and the children had suffered deeply. Before Daddy died, we'd had an abundance of everything we needed, but now it was a struggle to provide the necessities. Mother had taught herself to drive but never got her driver's license. She would not drive the speed limit, and traffic would be backed up a country mile. She had taken a job at a local cafe and also picked up odd jobs for extra income. My brother Billy had joined the army and served his country for two years. He sent money home to help out with the finances whenever he could. Harold had become the head of the family and was working a full-time job. My younger brothers, Russell and Danny, were attending school. My oldest sister cared for the younger children. I could see the sadness on their faces, and the pain of life without Daddy was very obvious. In the past, our home had always been filled with lots of children and laughter, but now it had become a very quiet, sober place. We were all trying to press forward. A lot had changed at the old home place.

My baby sister, Faye, was now attending the Alabama Institute for the Deaf in Talladega, Alabama. Mother had enrolled her when she was six years old. It was by far the hardest decision she'd ever made. It was a long way from home, and she had to leave her there. Mother wanted her to have a chance at a better life. She would learn many skills there that would open up a door of opportunity for her. Faye was too young to understand, and she thought Mother had abandoned her. Faye would come home for holidays and special occasions. As difficult as it was, we all knew it was preparing her for a prosperous future. Mother shed many tears missing that little girl.

Mother had no experience in finances, because Daddy had always taken care of everything. I don't think she had ever seen the inside of a bank before. It wasn't long until she lost the farm, because she couldn't pay the taxes. Life was hard, and she struggled to provide for her family.

When I got out of Draper, I felt like I had been given another chance at life. Dures Thomas, a lifelong friend to the Kilpatrick family, gave me an opportunity and opened doors for me. He gave me a job working at the Raccoon Mountain Kennels. Dures would go to trade day in Collinsville and buy dogs. Trade day was always on Saturday, and you could buy and trade almost anything. Dogs, knives, and watches were the most popular trading items. We sold fine-quality, high-class coon dogs and shipped them all over the country. We had a wide variety of Redbone, Bluetick, and Redtick dogs. We built the crates to ship them in, and we cleaned the pens every day. I also took care of a herd of ponies and worked in the chicken houses for Dures. It was good therapy working outside, working with my hands, and earning an honest day's pay. Freedom felt good. I had been given a second chance, and I was very grateful for all that Dures Thomas had done for me.

Ann had graduated from high school and was now working for her uncle, H. K. "Peck" Scott. She lived at home with her parents in Boaz, Alabama. It was one week before Christmas. I went to Gadsden with Ann, her parents, and her Aunt Erma. Broad Street was shining with Christmas lights, and every window was decorated with a Christmas theme. Music was playing on every corner, and I was in love. It was a beautiful, magical moment for me. I slipped into a jewelry store and bought Ann a string of pearls. Ann's aunt helped me pick them out. We also bought a real Christmas tree that day for Ann's parents. I thought it was the grandest tree I had ever seen. This would be a Christmas I would never forget and one that I would treasure.

I knew in my heart that Ann Scott was destined to be my wife. We were married on June 15, 1958, six months after my release from prison. We were married at Union Methodist Church in the community where I grew up. The Reverend Dossie Baker performed the ceremony. It was raining that day, but the sun was shining on my life. The woman I loved had waited all these years, and life had new meaning for me.

Dures Thomas built us a house and paid the deposits on all the utilities. Later he had a telephone installed for us. There were no words to thank him for the kindness and support he gave us during those years. He took me under his wing and treated me like his own son. I was overwhelmed by his generosity and genuine concern for me. For the first time since Daddy died, I felt as if I had a father figure in my life, someone looking out for me and someone I could trust.

In the spring of 1960, Ann and I found out we were expecting our first child. I was excited and nervous at the same time. Raising a child would be a huge responsibility, and I wasn't sure what kind of daddy I would be. I had no doubt that Ann would be a wonderful mother. On January 1, 1961, Marty Scott Kilpatrick was born. He was Marshall County's New Year's baby. I was so proud to be a daddy. I walked around with a silly grin on my face, chewing on a cigar. I handed out cigars to everyone who walked in the hospital that day, even the women. I had never experienced this kind of joy, and it was overwhelming. Ann had to stay in the hospital for a few extra days, because her blood was low. I was so excited the day I brought them home from the hospital. I drove the car up close to the back door so Ann wouldn't have far to walk. I couldn't wait to get my baby boy in the house and hold the "little dickens." I turned around, and Ann was coming in the back door, looking at me as if to say, "Gee, thanks for helping me get in the house." I was so anxious to hold Marty and check him out that I had completely forgotten about Ann. My heart was full of joy that day. This was a new season in our lives, and my heart was bursting with pride.

There was a small radio station across the street from our house. I had a buckskin mare that I rode up and down McVille Road in front of the radio station every day. One day, while I was out riding the mare with Marty in my lap, a fellow by the name of Beecher Hyde walked over from the radio station and introduced himself. Beecher was an announcer at the station. He politely said, "Are you not afraid that horse will get spooked and throw that baby out of your arms?" Marty was just a couple of months old at the time. I just smiled and said, "No." Beecher and I hit it off immediately, and we became good friends. I thought he had the most unusual name I had ever heard. It reminded me of Beech Nut chewing tobacco, which I enjoyed chewing very much. Ann and I would go out to eat with Beecher and his wife, Becky. One of our favorite places to eat was the Food Basket in Albertville. We shared a love for horses and went on many trail rides together. There was always laughter when Beecher was around. It was a friendship that I cherished for many years.

The following year, Dures sold some land across the street to a group of men who were interested in building a site for the Sand Mountain Saddle Club. These men were horsemen, and they enjoyed getting together, talking horses, riding horses, and hanging out with the horses. The first meeting was in 1961 at the home of Gene Holman. They started out with six members: Gene Holman, Gerald Thomas, J. B. Holsonback, Bud Despain, Vernon Brock, and Shirley Thomas. It wasn't long until other men wanted to join their club, so they needed to expand. They moved into a new location in 1962, and they met every Thursday night. I was invited to become a member, and, in 1964, I was voted in as the president of the club. It was a great honor for me. We went on trail rides and participated in the local Christmas parades. Later, we were able to build an arena to show horses. The club became a member of the Boaz

Chamber of Commerce. The saddle club would later begin sponsoring a ride for St. Jude's Children's Hospital. The money raised would be given for research. Donald Thomas went on to start "A Special Day for Special People," which was inspired by the son of a coworker. It was a day set aside for anyone with physical or mental disabilities. We would furnish a meal, a cowboy hat, a T-shirt, and a bandana. We also had a live band, and we took them on a wagon ride. It was a great day for all who participated. The Sand Mountain Saddle Club and its members have always had a heart for children. I felt comfortable around my new friends at the saddle club. They were my kind of people. The members of that club opened a door of opportunity for me to walk back into society and allowed me to be a part of something very special.

The year I was president of the saddle club, we went on our annual trail ride from Boaz, Alabama, to Altoona, Alabama. A lot of different saddle clubs participated in the ride. I was riding Smoky, a beautiful palomino stud, and Ann was riding Sunshine, a palomino mare. Ann was not a horse lover like me, but she knew how much I enjoyed the rides, and I was very proud to have her by my side. As we approached our campsite, I looked back over my shoulder and saw the most beautiful sight. The sun was just beginning to set, and behind me over a hundred people were riding horses or wagons. It was a perfect day, and I thought to myself that life couldn't get much better than this.

When Mr. Harvey Roebuck passed away, the saddle club members allowed me to lead his horse, Cannonball, around the arena. The horse was saddled with Mr. Harvey's boots in the stirrups backward, signifying a fallen rider. It was a memorial to the man we all loved and admired. He had been a special part of my life since I was a young boy. When I was young, I helped him cut wood, and I could sit and listen to his stories all day. Some days we didn't cut much wood, but I went home with his stories dancing in my mind. He was a godly man and dearly loved.

Ann and I established some lifelong friendships with members of the saddle club. Thomas and Gail Smith were among those friends. We went on trail rides together and spent many weekends hanging out at one another's homes. There was a special bond among us, and Thomas made me laugh. I owned a beautiful chestnut palomino horse named Smoky. Thomas thought it was a pretty thing, and he always wanted to buy the horse. One day, he told me to name my price, and I did. He bought my horse and then decided he wanted to register Smoky in a horse show, and he asked me if I would ride him in the show. I was honored to, and we won first place. I enjoyed the times we spent together and the good memories we made.

Marty was toddling around by now and getting into everything. We bought him his first dog, a German Shepherd named Bo Bo. German Shepherds are very protective dogs. Whenever Marty would walk toward the road, Bo Bo would grab him by the pant leg and pull him back toward the house. He took every step that Marty took. When Marty was in trouble, I would have to hide from Bo Bo to spank him. If he thought I was hurting Marty, he would tear into me. They were buds, and Bo Bo looked out for him.

I bought Marty a pony named Daisy Mae, and she was a pretty little thing. I would have her saddled up and waiting for him every morning in the hall of the dog kennel. I taught him to ride by the time he could walk. He showed her when he was two years old. I always hesitated about letting him participate in the horse shows. I usually judged them, and I did not want people to think I was being unfair, so I never gave him first place, even though he deserved it. Daisy Mae had been in so many horse shows that she automatically knew when to stop, go, and turn around. Mr. O. D. Bryant was a Cherokee Indian who helped me train the horses. He would always tell me that Marty could ride better than most men. I was proud of him, and I often wondered what Aubrey Kilpatrick would have thought about his grandson. He was a pistol and a little bit mischievous. He liked to get the water hose and spray the dogs when he helped me in the kennels. He knew I was going to whip him, but he would do it anyway.

Ann thought she would like to have six boys, but I decided one was a handful. I always feared for Ann and Marty's safety. In the back of my mind, I had a feeling that they were always in harm's way. The past would always come back to haunt me, and I would never be free from it. That played an important role in my decision to not have any more children.

Dures Thomas sold Raccoon Kennels to Charles Cooley. Charles moved the kennels to the Mountainboro community and changed the name to Sandy Downs.

He built a quarter-mile racetrack for horse races. He raced Quarter Horses and Thoroughbreds, and he also hosted rodeos. Charles asked me to work for him at Sandy Downs, and I was certainly glad he offered me the job. Billy also went to work there. Ann and I moved to Mountainboro so I could be closer to my job. I was one of the first men in the state to receive a license to start race horses and to monitor the race from start to finish.

Big Jim Folsom would send his aides to buy coon dogs from me. Word of mouth was the best advertisement for us. Charles advertised in sports magazines. It didn't take long for business to start booming. I was so excited to be a part of everything going on at Sandy Downs.

Preston Folkes owned a rodeo company. He would bring the rodeo stock on Monday and leave them so they would be rested for the rodeo on Saturday. Mr. Folkes had a son named Preston, Jr. Preston, Jr., was going to compete in the steer-wrestling competition at the rodeo, also known as bulldogging. It was an event in which a horse-mounted rider would chase a steer, drop from the horse onto the steer, and then wrestle the steer to the ground by twisting its horns. Preston, Sr., asked me if I knew anyone who had a fast horse to haze for Preston, Jr., because he wanted to bulldog in the rodeo. I told him I would haze for him, and Preston, Sr., wanted to know what I was going to ride. I told him I had a Southern Dixie mare that was very fast, and I showed him the horse. Preston, Sr., had a gray horse that Preston, Jr., was going to ride, and he told me he didn't think my little mare could keep up with his gray horse. I made a bet with him. I told him we would race, and if I had to turn around and yell "Come on, Preston!" he had to give me his gray horse; if he won, I would give him my Southern Dixie. Charles McDaniel was standing there, and he told Preston he was about to lose his horse, so we called off the bet and instead raced just for fun. About halfway through the race, I turned around and yelled, "Come on, Preston!" I crossed the finish line, turned around, and was headed back before he crossed the line. He was relieved that we'd called off the bet. I enjoyed many good times at Sandy Downs and met some very interesting people.

At one of the rodeos, Marty's cousin Tonya was there visitng. We were all standing around in the barn, talking to the cowboys and waiting for the rodeo to start. The cowboys were always putting Marty up to mischief. He liked spraying things with the water hose. There was a monkey that performed at the rodeo. It wore a little hat and rode around on the back of an Old English Sheepdog. While we were all standing around, the monkey jumped in Marty's lap, wrapped its arms around his neck, and wouldn't let go. Marty had this frightful look on his face, and Tonya laughed until she cried. Marty, on the other hand, did not find it humorous. We all had a good laugh.

Charles took us boys to Mississippi to buy a load of horses. They were called "killer" horses because they were wild, crazy, and out of control. You could buy them dirt cheap. I didn't buy any, because I knew they would never be broken, and someone would end up getting killed. Charles was mad at me for not buying any, so he took S. J. and went back to Mississippi and bought forty-two of those horses. I didn't know anything about it until they came back. The driver delivered them by way of a semi-tractor trailer. When they arrived at Sandy Downs, I looked at them and told the driver there was one good horse out of the whole bunch, and it was the black horse. The driver said, "That's my horse, and I brought him along in case I needed help with these crazy horses." One of the horses was a Lightning Bar horse, and I bet Charles $200 that the horse would never tote a saddle. I put a saddle on him, girded it up, opened the gate, and turned it loose. The horse went crazy and left its hoof print in the saddle. I won the bet. We loaded up the horses and headed to Kentucky to the horse sale. The owner of the horse sale had been asking us to bring some horses to his sale for over a year. When we arrived, we registered the horses and told the auctioneer that if anyone bids on them, they're buying them! Charles made me represent them, against my will. He said, "That's what I'm paying you for." I called them the mother-in-law horses. If you don't like your mother-in-law, just buy her one of these horses! Two men who worked with us were going to show the horses. They had both been drinking most of the day. One of them passed out, so we put him in the back of the horse trailer and covered him up with horse blankets. I'm surprised he didn't freeze to death, because there were three inches of snow on the ground, and it was bone-chillingly cold. The other man, Brent, said he would show the horses. Someone helped him get on the first horse, and the thing went crazy. It bucked and kicked and disrupted everything. It kicked its front feet over the top rail and went all the way around the pen. Brent was hanging on for dear life, and his legs were out in a V. That was the funniest sight I had ever seen. We sold every one of those "killer" horses, and I couldn't believe people were paying good money for them. About a month went by, and we received a phone call from the owner of the horse sale in Kentucky. He was upset and told Charles that he had wives, doctors, and lawyers calling and threatening to sue him because of the men who had been hurt by those crazy horses. He told Charles we were welcome to come to his sale anytime, but we could never run another horse through his sale. This old country boy from Alabama knew more about horses than they realized.

Charles took me to Florida with him to buy some horses, and while we were there, we went to the dog tracks. Charles wanted me to bet on the dogs, but I wouldn't, so he got me a pass to go in the pits. He wanted me to watch the dogs as they brought them out and tell him which ones to bet on. I could tell a lot about a dog by the way he was built. I looked at their heads, shoulders, muscles, and reach. In the first six races, I picked first-, second-, and third-place winners in all six races. Charles disagreed with one of the dogs I picked. He said the dog was too tall, but during the race he rolled the dogs that were in first and second place and went on to win the race! Charles was a very wealthy, happy man that day. He won enough money to pay for the load of horses we bought, plus our room and meals for the trip. Picking and choosing dogs and horses was a gift handed down from my daddy, or maybe it was just a natural gift. It came as naturally as breathing.

One of my favorite memories at Sandy Downs was the year four men from Kentucky came looking for a "meat dog." That is a dog that will tree anything and everything. The men did not have an appointment; they just showed up. I had a man from Chicago who was scheduled to arrive that same day. The four men told me what they were looking for in a dog and asked if I had anything. I showed them one of our best dogs. They wanted to try him out before they bought him, so I had to find them a place to hunt. I told them if they didn't like the dog, they could bring it back early the next morning, and I would reimburse their money. The next morning, before daylight, they pulled down the long driveway to Sandy Downs, going about five miles an hour. When they stopped the car, they opened the doors, and they all fell out. They were drunk, and the dog was sitting in the front seat of the car. I thought they were not satisfied with the dog and had brought him back. When I asked them what the problem was, they replied, "That is the best dog in the whole world. He treed two coons, three possums, and then the dog started trailing again and fell in a hole. Inside the hole was five gallons of whiskey! We just had to come back and thank you personally. Money won't buy a dog like that! Not only is he a meat dog, but he'll get you something to drink as well." The men were pleased not only with the dog but also with our Southern hospitality.

George Elrod helped me out at Sandy Downs from time to time. George was one of the most intelligent men I'd ever met. He had a lot of book knowledge and wisdom about horses. I was breaking a horse one day, and George was offering me advice from one of his books. The horse was bucking and pitching a fit. George yelled out something, and I yelled back, "Read louder, George! The horse isn't listening!" I didn't have any book knowledge about horses, but I had heart knowledge. I was always fascinated with horses and their wild spirit. There were times that I would just sit and talk to them like they were my best friends. Some people say that the dog is man's best friend. To some I guess that's true, but for me, the horse was my best friend. There is no animal more graceful and beautiful than a horse.

J. T. Poole was a bachelor who lived in Leeds, Alabama, with his elderly dad on a cattle farm. J. T.'s dad said a man would be crazy to own a stud horse, and he did not allow J. T. to buy one. J. T. asked me to bring a stud horse out to their farm to breed with his mares. I took my horse Mekko Star out to their farm and left him. While my horse was there, the elderly man took up with the horse. Every day, Mr. Poole would take stale bread and feed the horse out of his hand. Mekko Star would follow him down to the creek. He also had a cattle dog that befriended my stud horse. The old man, the horse, and the dog became buddies. J. T. called me and said he needed to get up some cows to take to the sale. I told him to ride Mekko Star, but he said he was too old and could not stay on him when he got to cutting out cows. I told him to ride the horse, cut the cow out at a walk, and then get off and use his dog and hang the reins over the saddle horn. The dog and the horse would run the cow to the barn, and the dog would keep it there until the horse came back to get J. T. It was entertaining to watch that horse and dog work together. When the work was finished, J. T. asked me if I would sell him my stud horse and so I did. Mr. Poole told him he couldn't sell Mekko until he died. Some people never realize how attached they can become to an animal. The old man had a new best friend, and it was a stud horse named Mekko Star.

In the years I worked at the dog kennels, I sold over 2,500 dogs and shipped them all over the world. I broke horses, traded horses, showed horses, and participated in rodeos. Working at Raccoon Mountains and Sandy Downs was good therapy for me. I enjoyed those years and the men I was honored to work with. Ann and I made many new friends during those years. It was a great environment for Marty to grow up in.

It all came naturally and easy for this country boy. My life has been full of memories like these, and I will cherish them all until I die.

"If God be for us, who can be against us?"   *(Romans 8:31   KJV)*

CHAPTER SEVEN:
REDEEMING LOVE

Ann's uncle, H. K. Scott, offered me a job driving a gas truck. It would mean more money and benefits, so I accepted the job. This would allow us to build a new house next door to Ann's parents. In 1967, we moved into our new home in the Smith Institute community, next door to Orb and Tiny Scott. We were excited about all the changes in our lives.

Living next door to Orb and Tiny Scott gave me a sense of belonging and a peace I couldn't describe. I enjoyed being in their company. They played an important role in our lives, and they adored their only grandchild. Orb and Marty were best buds, and they were attached at the hip. Some of my fondest memories are days sitting on their front porch, sharing stories and enjoying sweet fellowship with Orb Scott. Orb and Tiny had become a part of our everyday life, and they treated me like a son.

Ann had given her heart to Christ at the tender age of twelve and was a member of Liberty Baptist Church in Dekalb County. Tiny Scott was a member of the Belcher's Methodist Church, which was also located in Dekalb County. They were both godly women who were faithful to the Lord. I was not a churchgoing man and neither was my father-in-law. We would sit on the porch and tell stories while the women went to church on Sundays. One Sunday evening, I could tell something was bothering Ann; later that night, she shared her faith with me. She expressed how deeply she cared for me. She wanted me to get saved, receive Christ, and go to church with her and Marty. Ann said that God would draw me, and, when he did, I should accept him.

I could tell it was weighing heavy on her heart. I listened, and I let it penetrate into my heart, but I didn't do anything about it.

Ted Scott, Ann's first cousin, was an ordained minister and the pastor at Whitesboro Baptist Church. Ted also worked for Peck Scott at S. & W. tire shop beside the San Ann service station. The church was having a summer revival, and Ted had invited the family to attend. He came and talked to me on Tuesday evening and personally invited me to church at Whitesboro's revival. Ted shared with me about the love of God. I was already under conviction, and his words penetrated into my heart and soul. Later I learned that Ann had asked him to talk to me. On Friday night, our family loaded up and went to the revival at Whitesboro. When we walked in, I could feel a stirring down in my heart. It seemed that everyone was happy in that place. People were singing about the goodness of God, and some people stood and shared a testimony about what God had been doing in their lives. Then Robert Jones, the evangelist, stood up and preached. He preached about a place called hell, and it seemed the whole time he was preaching, he was looking at me! Something was going on in that place, and I was getting excited on the inside. When the evangelist invited people to come and receive Christ, my father-in-law, Orb Scott, was one of the first to go to the altar. Right behind him was Brent Cofield. The altar was full that night, and many people were saved. This was the happiest bunch of people I had ever been around, and I wanted what they had. I could sense something different in my father-in-law, and I was excited about it. I wanted to go forward that night, too, but something held me back.

Before the service was dismissed that night, Ted made an announcement. He invited everyone to come back the following night, which was Saturday. Revival was supposed to end on Friday, but he felt strongly about extending it another night. He said he might be the only one to show up, but he promised he would be there the following night.

The following day, I had to work, driving the gas truck. It had been a restless night, and I was remembering a lot of things from my past.

I pulled up at the San Ann service station in Boaz with a load of gas early that morning. When I got out of the truck, I felt a presence unlike anything I had ever felt. It was a tugging from the Holy Spirit of God. He was drawing me to him, and I remembered the words of my wife: "He will draw you, and, when he does, I want you to accept him." I walked around to the back of the gas truck, knelt down, and asked Christ to come into my heart. I confessed my sins, and he was quick to forgive them. He washed me in his precious blood and set my feet on a firm foundation. I couldn't wait to get to revival at Whitesboro Baptist Church that night. I didn't know whether to laugh or cry. God had rescued me and restored all that had been lost. When we walked in the doors of that little country church, I thought I might have a running fit. I contained myself, and then there was an opportunity, and I seized the moment. I stood and shared with the congregation and my family what the Lord had done for me. Talk about some happy folks. I now had that happiness and joy flooding my soul. My eyes were opened, my sins forgiven, and my past was under the blood. This country boy was a sinner saved by grace. That same night, I went forward and joined the church.

Dock Gaskin owned some land in the Whitesboro community, and he was also a member of Whitesboro Baptist Church. He allowed the church to have baptisms in his pond. On a warm Sunday afternoon, Ted Scott and Brown Hallmark baptized me in the name of the Father, the Son, and the Holy Spirit, and they called me brother. I was now a member of the family of God, and I had never known such love. I went down in that muddy water as an orphan, but I came up a child of God! I remembered being a boy without a daddy, a son without a father, and a man with no inheritance. I was now a man clothed with royalty and given an inheritance from my Heavenly Father. I could not believe the changes that were taking place in my heart and life.

Orb Scott, my father-in-law, joined the Belcher's Methodist Church where his wife, Tiny, was already a member. Reverend Ebb Cryar was the pastor, and he baptized Orb. God had heard and answered the prayers of our wives. One Sunday afternoon a few weeks later, we were all sitting out on the porch at Orb and Tiny's house, and out of nowhere, Marty asked, "What is the difference between the Baptist and the Methodist?" We all looked at one another, and then his mother said, "Well, the Baptist is just a little bit better than the Methodist." We all laughed, and I thought to myself, *what a difference a day can make.*

It wasn't long after I became a Christian that Marty came forth and gave his heart to Christ. I walked down to the altar with him, and we prayed. When we got up, I could see his tears on the altar. I started to wipe them away, but instead I decided to let them dry there. Talk about a proud papa; my cup had runneth over. Marty joined Whitesboro Baptist Church and was baptized in the same pond where I had been baptized. I was so proud of him and so amazed that God loved me enough to save me and my son.

I wanted everyone to get saved, especially my family. I was so excited about what God had done and was doing in my life. The first person I ever witnessed to was my mother. I got down on my knees in front of her and shared Jesus with her and my brothers and sisters. Some of them listened, and some walked out of the room. I know they thought I had lost my mind, but I didn't care. I went home that night and began praying for God to deal with them and draw them to him. God in all his mercy heard my prayers, and eventually they all accepted the Lord. Russell had already given his heart to Christ at the age of twelve at Union Methodist Church.

My brother Billy was saved at Unity Baptist Church the following year. I don't know who was happier the night Billy got saved, him or me. I was so excited that I turned around and picked Ann's cousin Ted up into the air and twirled him around. Ted was about six feet tall, and I was a little man, but the power of the Lord was in me that night, and I felt like there was nothing I couldn't do with the help of the Lord. Soon after that, Billy announced his call to preach and later on started a Christian radio broadcast in Boaz, Alabama, on WBSA. Billy felt the call to invest in the radio broadcast. It cost $35.00 a week, and he needed sponsors. I joined Billy at the broadcast and became a sponsor. God had heard my prayers, and he was saving my family.

Sunday had become my favorite day of the week. I was still driving the gas truck at San Ann for Ann's uncle, Peck Scott. I had to work every Sunday, but my heart longed to be at the radio broadcast with Billy and in church with my family. I talked to Peck about letting me off on Sundays, and he offered me a job in the cigarette warehouse. He also gave me a side job helping out at his farm in Sand Valley, Alabama. Peck owned a grand piece of land in the valley, and he had two hundred head of Black Angus cattle grazing in the pasture. It was a beautiful, peaceful place, and I enjoyed working there. I was so thankful to be off on Sundays, and it was a blessing that I would never take for granted.

I helped Billy with the broadcast, and a few years later he handed it down to me and started sponsoring another broadcast in the Albertville area. The broadcast was a way we could share our love of Christ with others. It was also an opportunity to help young preachers just starting out. God had given me a second chance and an opportunity to work in his kingdom. I wanted to extend that message to everyone with whom I came into contact. The opening song to the broadcast was "Tell Me the Story of Jesus." I wanted everyone to know this man called Jesus. I stood amazed every day that he loved me enough to give his life on an old rugged cross. Sometimes when Billy was preaching, my mind would drift back to the time when we were just young boys, and God would remind me that he had brought us safe thus far. God had put a hedge of protection around us on May 17, 1951, because he knew that this day would come, a day when we would receive him as Lord of our lives. It had been a long, hard journey for our family, but God had not forsaken us.

Mr. Hershel Wofford co-hosted the radio broadcast with me after Billy left. He sponsored and supported me until the day he went home to be with Jesus. I loved that man and the influence he had on so many people. I visited him at his home the day he was dying. I noticed that a little bird would fly to his window and then fly away. A few minutes later, it would come back, sit for a while, and look in the window. After my brother in Christ drew his last breath, the bird never returned. I believe it was a little messenger from God, reminding Brother Hershel that God takes care of the sparrows and he will take care of you. It was a peaceful journey from this side to God's paradise. I stayed with the family until the funeral home came for the body. I lost a dear friend that day, but I had the blessed assurance that I would see him again someday.

God sent sponsors and support for the radio broadcast each Sunday morning. Walter Smith, Joe Sutherland, Marlon Smith, Buddy Claborn, Wayne Roden, and so many more helped me with the program. Reverend Billy Painter preached for me every second Sunday, and Patty Handley would sing. Patty was like my daughter; she called me Papa, and she had a special place in my heart. She was always faithful about being there for me. Reverend Wayne White had a standing appointment with us every fourth Sunday. After my buddy Hershel Wofford passed, the church at Bethlehem came along beside me and became a sponsor. My cousin George Kilpatrick and his wife, Carolyn, were also sponsors. The broadcast became my heartbeat, my way of giving back to the Lord. I could never repay his mercy and grace, but I could love him and serve him. My testimony was simple: "In spite of what anyone has done, there is forgiveness. My desire is that men, women, boys, and girls come to know the Lord." I was not an ordained preacher, but I had been commanded by the Lord to be a witness and a soul winner for Jesus Christ.

"And ye shall seek me and find me, when ye shall search for me with all your heart." (Jer. 29:13 KJV)

CHAPTER 8:
FORGIVENESS, HEALING,
AND RESTORATION

Life had new meaning, and I cherished every day as a gift from God. For many years, I had harbored hate and anger against the men who were responsible for the death of my daddy. I blamed them for my years in prison and the hardship it had caused my family. After I gave my life to Christ, my pastor and friend, Ted Scott, encouraged me to read God's word. He said the scriptures would lead, guide, and direct my path. I took his advice and began to read the word of God. One night, as I was reading, these scriptures seemed to jump off the page and pierce deep into my soul: "For if you forgive men their trespasses, your Heavenly Father will also forgive you: but if you forgive not men their trespasses, neither will your Father forgive your trespasses" (Matthew 6:14-15 KJV). Tears began to fall, and the spirit of God convicted me. At that moment, I asked God to help me forgive my enemies and to remove the hate in my heart. It did not happen overnight, and it was a slow process. The hate and anger had been building in me for years, but God was changing and transforming me. Satan had almost destroyed my life, but Jesus died to save me and give me eternal life. The word says, "Love your enemies, bless them that curse you, do good to them that hate you, and pray for them that despitefully use you and persecute you" (Matthew 5:44 KJV).

God set my feet on a firm foundation at Whitesboro Baptist Church. I grew in the wisdom and knowledge of the Lord. God planted a seed in my heart to help build the Beth Haven Baptist Church. Several families had talked to me and Ann about investing our time, money, and spiritual gifts into the new church. The vision became a reality, and I thought that we would be there forever, but a new season was springing up in our lives. God had another plan, and we began searching out his will for our lives. The word of God says, "To every thing there is a season, and a time to every purpose under the heaven" (Ecc. 3:1 KJV). Ann and I visited several churches before God led us to Bethlehem Baptist Church. Reverend Wayne White was the pastor, and good things were happening in the church. God was being glorified through the music, the testimonies, and the word of God. Souls were being won to Christ, and the church was growing. I remember the day Brother Wayne and a committee from the church came to my home. They asked me if I would consider becoming a deacon of the church. I felt so unworthy that I dropped my head in shame. Brother Wayne reminded me that none of us are worthy of the honor and privilege to work in the kingdom, but because Christ died, we are given that opportunity. It was the most humbling moment of my life, and I accepted the offer and was ordained a deacon. Bethlehem was home, and we were there to stay. Every day of my life has been a reminder of the goodness and love of God. Only by his grace have I made it this far. I am still amazed that he loved a wretch like me. "Behold what manner of love the Father hath bestowed upon us, that we should be called the sons of God." (1 John 3:1 KJV)

A lot of changes took place in our lives over the course of fifty years. We eventually left San Ann and took other jobs. Ann went to work for the Coca-Cola Company in Albertville, and I took a job at Yvonne Smith's cabinet shop. A year later, Mr. Smith sold me the business, and I moved the Kilpatrick Wood Shop to our home. God had blessed us, and now he was giving us an opportunity to bless others. I was able to hire several young men to help me in the cabinet shop over the years. Among them were Tim and David Feemster, William and Jim Renfro, Butch and J. T. Cartee, Tony Gregory, Ronald Hayes, Ryan McPherson, and more. It was more than an opportunity to teach them a trade; it was a chance to be a witness for Christ in front of them. Unfortunately, they would witness the good, the bad, and the ugly sides of me from time to time. I still struggled with my temper, and I could not tolerate liars and thieves. Lazy people tried my patience, and I was a perfectionist. My wife and son could vouch for this. There were days I was not an easy man to live with or work for. Every time I messed up, God would pick up the broken pieces and mold me back together. I was just clay in the potter's hands, and he was still trying to mold me into a better man.

God was providing for our every need, and the cabinet shop made a good income for our family. A few years later, a chicken farm just down the road from us came up for sale. The farm had a chicken house, a farmhouse, and several acres of land. Ann and I didn't know a thing about raising chickens, but we would soon learn. The chicken houses were old and needed a lot of work. Later on, we were able to build two new chicken houses on our land. We hired J. W. and Joann Kirkland to help us. They were honest, dependable, and hardworking folks. Ann eventually retired from Coca-Cola, and I got out of the cabinet business. Raising horses and chickens kept us busy. Ann later took a part-time job at the Albertville Memorial and Etowah Memorial funeral homes. She also worked at Carr Funeral Home from time to time, and I would help her. The blessings of God were overflowing in our lives.

I had always been and always would be a horseman. I began riding, breaking, and trading horses when I was just a young boy. Horses would always be a part of my life. We raised Quarter Horses and Paint Horses. During a good season, we would breed around fifty to sixty horses. Champ was my stud Quarter Horse, and Skip was my stud Paint Horse. That bloodline had been around for years, and they were part of the family. I was at peace with the world when I was riding and working with my horses.

The good Lord had blessed us abundantly. We owned our home and a beautiful piece of land, and we were able to have our own business at home. Life was good, and I would look out at all the Lord had given me, and I would remember where I was and where I came from. But most important, I would remember where I was going. Sometimes I would get so excited that I would sing "Amazing Grace" while walking through the hall of the barn, and it felt like I was walking on holy ground. God had surrounded me with a good family, good friends, and a wonderful church family. I could not begin to count my blessings. Jesus loved me, died for me, and saved me. I am still amazed at the redeeming love of Christ. I remind myself every day that I am just an old sinner saved by grace.

Let me speak honestly. From time to time, my cardinal man would drift back to May 17, 1951, and I could feel the anger resurfacing, but then Jesus would gently draw me back into his word, and he would remind me of his forgiveness toward me.

"Let all bitterness, and wrath, and anger, and clamour, and evil speaking, be put away from you, with all malice: and be ye kind one to another, tenderhearted, forgiving, one another, even as God for Christ's sake hath forgiven you." (Ephesians 4:31-32 KJV)

CHAPTER 9:
FATHERS AND SONS

Through the years, the times I spent with my son were some of my fondest memories. I remember his first step, his first word, and sitting him on his first pony. I remember his first puppy, first whipping, and that first date. But more important than all these things, I remember when he walked down an aisle in an old-fashioned church, knelt at an old-fashioned altar, and asked Jesus into his heart. That was the best moment of this daddy's life. I knew at that very moment no matter what happened in Marty's life, the Lord would be there to help him through it. The word of God says, "Train up a child in the way he should go; and when he is old he will not depart from it" (Proverbs 22:6 KJV). I held on to that scripture, and I claimed it for my son.

I look back sometimes and wonder if I was too hard on Marty. My daddy was hard on me and expected a lot out of me, and in some ways I was a lot like my daddy. I worked him hard, and I didn't tolerate laziness. I wanted to teach Marty the value of working hard and earning the respect of others. When I was working, Marty was always helping me. It didn't matter what I was doing or where I was; I expected him to be there, too. We would vaccinate the cattle at Peck Scott's farm, K & K Farms in Big Wills Valley. He helped me on weekends and during the summer. The farm was a place of beauty and serenity, and I felt at peace when I was there working with my son. My father-in-law, Orb, also helped out from time to time, and he stood watch over the place.

I had a Quarter Horse named Meeko Poco and an Australian Sheppard dog that I took to the farm to help me round up the cattle. All I had to do was whistle, and they would round up the cattle and run them into the holding pen. We used a head-catch on the cow, and then I would straddle it and vaccinate it. We would work from dawn to dusk. We would break for lunch and go down to the local country store and buy Beanie Weenies and crackers. The store was the local gathering place where all the retired old-timers hung out and told their stories. When we went into the store, they would ask us if we were vaccinating cows, and by the time we got back to the farm, they would all be there to watch. The men were astonished at the horse and dog and how they knew what to do just from hearing me whistle. It was a way to pass the time and entertaining to them. It always reminded me of the times when my brothers and I were young boys. We would go to the local store and break wild mules and ride them home. All the old-timers would gather around to watch.

During Marty's young-adult years, we began participating in Rodeo Team Roping. It was a sport that involved horsemen roping steers. We would practice on Tuesday and Thursday nights and then compete on Friday and Saturday nights. It was good, quality time between father and son. Our love for horses and the competition was common ground for us. We grew very close during those years, and I cherished every moment. I knew that these days would slip away too quickly.

Marty got married and adopted a beautiful, bright-eyed little girl named Johannah. A few years later, on July 3, 2000, Marty's son, Justin, was born. Ann and I were so excited to be grandparents. We bought each of them a pony, and I enjoyed leading the ponies around to let them ride. They were both a little fearful, but they knew I would never let anything hurt them. Justin would sit in my lap and drive my old blue truck around the house. They brought much happiness into our lives. Several years later, we had the privilege of becoming grandparents to three more boys, Andrew, Brandon, and Caleb. Boys are always getting into something. One day, Justin and Caleb were in the hall of the barn, riding a little donkey bareback, and it was bucking and pitching a fit. They were holding on for dear life. That was a funny sight to behold, and we all had a good belly laugh. God's word says, "A merry heart doeth good like a medicine" (Proverbs 17:22 KJV). Children can turn your bitter heart into a happy heart. My grandchildren have been good medicine. "Children's children are the crown of old men; and the glory of children are their fathers" (Proverbs 17:6 KJV). I am so thankful that God brought these precious children into our life, and I praise the Lord that they all came to know Christ.

As I look at my son today, I am reminded of the joy he has brought to me and how proud I am to be his daddy. I know that Aubrey Kilpatrick would have been proud to have him as a grandson. Sometimes I wonder how different our lives would be if Daddy were still here. Now that I am older, I can see more clearly that God knows what is best for a person, and he directs our path.

"And all thy children shall be taught of the Lord; and great shall be the peace of thy children." (Isaiah 54:13KJV)

CHAPTER 10:
FAMILIES AND GOODBYES

Ann and I both had strong family ties, and each year our families would have a reunion. Here in the South, we like family reunions, high-school reunions, and any other reunion as long as there is food involved. A traditional family reunion for us was a day packed with good fellowship, stories of yesterday, pony rides, and a large meal fit for a king. My favorite part of the day was the pony rides. I would lead the pony while the children rode. It did my heart good to see their smiles and hear their laughter. I would always stop somewhere during the day and reflect back on where I had been and where I was going. My life had been an amazing journey, and the good Lord had blessed me abundantly.

I would think about Daddy and wonder what he would think about the heritage he had left behind. He would get a kick out of all his children and grandchildren. He would be so proud of the men and women his sons and daughters had become, and he would be honored to be a part of their lives. Sometimes, it made me very sad to stop and realize all that Aubrey Kilpatrick had missed.

I was very thankful for the mother that God had given me. She had sacrificed much as a young widow after the untimely death of my daddy. After forty years, she would still sit and cry, longing for the days of her youth and the man she loved. There would always be a void in her life that no one else could ever fill. She had never completely recovered after losing Daddy. Elizabeth Kilpatrick loved her children and her grandchildren. I could never repay Mother for standing by my side, fighting for me until the end, and never giving up on me. A mother's love is like the love of God. A good mother loves her children unconditionally, just as our Heavenly Father loves us.

Orb and Tiny Scott—the very mention of their names brings a smile to my face and warmth to my heart. They loved me like a son and had always treated me with kindness and respect. I could never put into words what they meant to me and how much I loved them. The Scott and Amos families had always treated me like blood kin, and I was a better man because of them.

In March of 1987, Tiny Scott went home to be with the Lord. Three years later, in March of 1990, Orb Scott joined her. In September of 1990, my mother, Elizabeth Kilpatrick, closed her eyes in death and was finally at peace. I knew they were all home with Jesus and reunited with family and friends, but my heart ached for them. They had all been constants in my life and part of the strong foundation I had built my life on. They had all loved me and believed in me, and it was hard to let them go.

For most of my life, I had been a strong, hardworking, healthy man. I had always taken pride in the fact that I could work circles around the young men who worked for me. In 1997, I began to notice a change in my body. At first, it was noticeable when I walked. My feet and legs seemed to move in slow motion, and my hands would tremble from time to time. I could sense that my body and mind were not working together. I just shrugged it off until it became more noticeable, and then Ann and Marty insisted I see a doctor. In September 2001, I was diagnosed with Parkinson's disease. The news was hard for me to grasp. I did not want to be sick and become a burden to my family. I purposed in my heart that I would do everything in my power to overcome this disease and stay as healthy as I could. I refused to sit around feeling sorry for myself.

Parkinson's disease attacks the nervous system and progresses very slowly. The brain cells slowly degenerate, and the muscles become stiff and rigid. You lose the ability to make rapid, spontaneous movements, and eventually you lose your balance and mobility. That is a lot to comprehend at one time.

In the beginning, I was still able to work on the farm and take care of the chickens and horses. Working had always been therapy for me. Through it all, my greatest concern was the burden the disease would place on Ann and Marty as it progressed. I prayed and tried to turn it all over to God, but I still had fear and anxiety about our future. The hardest thing for a man to deal with is losing his independence and becoming dependent on others. It strips you of your dignity and pride. As the Parkinson's worsened, I was at the mercy of others, and I could feel my world fading away.

I had made preparations for this moment over forty years ago behind a gas truck at the San Ann gas station in Boaz. I cried out for mercy, and the Lord heard my cry. I gave my life to Christ, and I tried to live for him the best I could. In the midst of my anguish and despair, I did not fear death, but I feared leaving Ann behind. I was not ready to let her go.

Fast forward to November 25, 2009

Today, Parkinson's has taken over my body and mind, but it has not touched my soul. My family has been in and out all day. I can hear their voices and see their faces, but I can't communicate with them. My dearest Ann has stood by my side for fifty-one years, in sickness and in health. She has kept the promises she made to me on our wedding day. God sent her to rescue me in the darkest days of my life. She led me to Jesus and restored my hope. Her faith will see her through as we let go and say goodbye, for a little while.

This old body is very tired, and my eyes are growing dim. God blessed me with seventy-five years of life. He brought me from the gates of hell to the gates of glory, and today I will enter into sweet rest with Jesus, my faithful friend.

There will be another family reunion, and the children of God will rejoice forever more. If you haven't made preparations for that day, let me plead with you: Don't wait; get saved today. Farewell, my loved ones. God be with you until we meet again.

"For which cause we faint not, but though our outward man perish, yet the inward man is renewed day by day. For our light affliction, which is but for a moment, worketh for us a far more exceeding and eternal weight of glory. While we look not at things which are seen, but at things which are not seen, for the things which are seen are temporal, but the things which are not seen are eternal." (2 Cor. 4:16-18 KJV)

CONCLUSION:
THE HORSEMAN DEPARTS

James Kilpatrick loved the Lord with all his heart. He continued to attend church services at Bethlehem Baptist Church as long as he was able. I would watch him walk into the sanctuary, his body trembling and his feet moving in slow motion, but his spirit was singing. His life was an inspiration to all who knew him.

He will always have a special place in my heart. In the fall of 2004, we were having a picnic at our home with the children from the Alabama Baptist Children's Home in Decatur. Brother James and Ann brought their miniature horses and spent the day leading the horses while the children rode around the farm. The man loved children and horses, and they loved him. He was a rare and special breed, just like the horses he raised.

Brother James spent his last days in the Albertville Nursing Home. The disease was taking away his quality of life, but God was renewing his spirit. One day, while Ann was pushing him down the hall in his wheelchair, she stopped and asked him if he was ready to go back to his room. He replied, "No. It's time for the preaching. I'm not a preacher, but I have had a Christian radio program for the last thirty-five years. Open your Bibles to the book of Matthew." Then he shared the good news of Jesus Christ with anyone who would listen. That was not the last time he would share the Gospel. On Easter Sunday 2009, the First Baptist Church in Albertville came to the nursing home to have Sunday school and Communion service. Ann and James attended the service that morning. As the preacher was finishing up, Brother James asked Ann to push him to the pulpit, and then he asked everyone to gather around. Once again he said, "It's time for the preaching. Open your

Bibles to the book of John 7: 37-38. I was older when I got saved, but I wish I had been younger. Don't wait; get saved." Then he quoted these scriptures: "If any man thirst let him come unto me and drink. He that believeth on me, as the scripture hath said, out of his belly shall flow rivers of living water" (John 7:37-38 KJV).

James Kilpatrick continued to plead with lost humanity to get saved. He was faithful about sharing the Gospel on the radio broadcast for thirty-five years. He was not an ordained preacher, but he loved the Lord his God, and he shared the good news of Jesus with everyone he met.

On Father's Day 2009, Ann drove James to the radio broadcast for the last time. His friends were there to greet him.

On November 25, 2009, my brother in Christ left this old world and entered into God's paradise. He fought a good fight; he finished strong. Some believe he is preparing the white horses for the army of God. I can see him in his white robe, white cowboy hat, and shiny new cowboy boots. He will be missed.

The day of his funeral, after the body had been laid to rest, three horses trotted up to the fence across the street from the cemetery and stood at attention, as if they were saluting their fallen friend . . .

Dana Hill

REMEMBERING JAMES

I NEVER KNEW THAT THE summer I attended the trial of James Kilpatrick at the Albertville Court House would change my life forever. I guess you might say it was love at first sight for me. James was at the front of the court house, and I was all the way in the back, but the image of him stayed with me. After the trial that day, I met his mother, and she asked if I would write to him while he was in jail. I wrote him a letter and sent it to the city jail, not knowing he was in the county jail. Miraculously, he eventually received the letter and wrote me one back. That was the beginning of our love affair. For some reason, I could not get that boy out of my head.

James Kilpatrick had a funny side but also a very serious side. He accepted my family as his own, and he loved them dearly. The Scott family treated him like a son, not a son-in-law.

When James got saved, there was a big difference in him. He didn't use all those little "pet" words anymore. He enjoyed going to revivals and sharing the love of God on the radio broadcast. James felt like the radio broadcast was his call from God. He missed a program only for illness or the weather. We would lie in bed at night and talk about how good God had been to us and how blessed we were to have family, friends, and our church family.

My husband was neat with his clothes and especially his hair. People would always comment about him being a neat freak. We celebrated fifty-one years of marriage. There were good times, hard times, and some sad times. I wouldn't change one thing, but I wish we could have had another fifty years and him healthy. He fought Parkinson's with every fiber of his being. I wouldn't call him back, because I know where he is, and how great it is to know that the hard life he endured is finally behind him.

I remember when his brother Billy got saved. He walked over to James, and they walked to the altar together. When Billy came up and shared the good news that God had saved him, James got so excited that he picked my cousin Reverend Ted Scott up off the ground. James was a short man, and Ted was six feet tall. I can still visualize that. He was so happy that God was saving his family.
I will always love him, and I was so proud to be his wife.

Ann Scott Kilpatrick

Growing up the son of James Kilpatrick and the grandson of Aubrey Kilpatrick, I cannot say that life was one big, fun time. But then, who hasn't had hard times and bad times? I grew up with my father, who was a great dad but also a hard one. I could see that he did not have fear of anything, and I was supposed to be the same, even though I did have fear. If I was riding a horse and it started to show out in view of my dad, I knew that it was going to get a whipping and that I would be made to stay on the pony while he whipped it. I got several blows from a rope or whip that were meant for the horse. I knew it was not intentional, but it still hurt, and the horse bucking and rearing up did make me afraid.

I don't know the first time I was ever told about my father's life and the event of May 17, 1951. I guess my mom told me, since I was a momma's boy. I could go to her easily with anything, and she would have patience and understanding. My dad was more the type of person to take action, not use words. Over the years, I have been asked hundreds of times if I knew any of those Kilpatricks, or if I was kin to any of the ones involved. I have always answered honestly and spoken up that yes, that was my grandfather and my dad. I, like anyone who was affected by May 17, 1951, would love to have changed what happened. Many people lost their loved ones, I never got to meet my grandfather, and nothing good came from it. But I have never been ashamed of what my father did. To this day, I know he was protecting his family and did not know what was taking place other than that his own life and the lives of his family were in danger.

My dad loved kids, and I could not understand why he seemed so patient with other kids but was tough on me. I know now, and I would not change the way he was toward me. Maybe he knew a bit more about parenting than a lot of folks. Play growing up involved horses; my dad did not like sports of any kind. So when I was young, it was horses or work. Those were the two things we did together. Later, in school, I did play sports and had no issues about it from him. Unfortunately, this was the time in my life when we were not close. I regret that now.

I do remember when he got saved and made it public in church. I didn't know anything about salvation other than that it was a good thing and I wanted my daddy to have it. I remember Brown Hallmark talking to him that night at the church; sweat was running off of Brown onto Daddy's pant leg. I remember standing on the altar as people came around to shake his hand.

Later in life, we got into roping, and this was the best time of my life. We would rope together and buy and sell horses. Almost every evening was spent at the barn together. I miss those days. We really got close during this time, and I relive the memories every day.

Every Sunday morning, Daddy had a Christian radio broadcast. I would feed the chickens and take care of the chores so he could attend the broadcast. The broadcast was his heart.

In the last days, when Parkinson's was taking its toll, it was hard to look at him and see what the disease had done to the man who'd had no fear and had always been stronger than any man I had ever known. I just could not believe that something could change a person's physical makeup that much. It was hard to see him go but almost a relief at the same time, for I know he would not have wanted to be in the shape he was in. I remember the funeral and a comment that was made by one of the ministers. He said, "I guess God needed him right now to help get those white horses ready for the Lord's return. I know he is taking good care of them, and he is in the arms of God."

See you soon, Dad,
Marty Scott Kilpatrick

There is a saying, "The eyes are the windows into the soul," and the Bible tells us, "The lamp of the body is the eye." When I think about James, I see his eyes. His eyes held an expression of happy contentment in the present circumstances. It is a trait that my husband inherited, and I see James most in him through this. This was most noticeable to me when he was with family and friends, especially children. When Marty and I married and three grandsons were added to the family, one of the first things James did was buy them a horse. I am grateful they were able to know him. I have known James for thirty years. One of the traits I admired most is that he knew a lot about a lot; however, he was not compelled to make sure everyone was aware of it. When he did talk, what he said was informative and important. No wasted words were spoken. He could also tell a story with great wit and humor, and it was a treat to listen when he did. This is also a trait Marty inherited, and I see his dad in him during those moments. I am grateful for the time I had with James and honored to be his daughter-in-law. When asked (and it happens often) "Which Kilpatricks are you related to?" I am very proud to say that I am Marty's wife, that Ann is my mother-in-law, and that James Kilpatrick was my father-in-law.

Rhonda Brand Kilpatrick

Papa always had candy and bubble gum, and I knew where he hid it. He bought me a pony named Trixie. He would saddle it up for me and lead her around while I rode her. I spent more quality time with him in the summer when I was out of school.

The thing I admired most about Papa was the way he handled his sickness. When he got sick with Parkinson's, he still got up in the morning, got dressed, and went outside. He still had a will to live, and he made the best of each day. That is what I will always remember.

Johannah Kilpatrick

When you are born into a family, they are stuck with you. Stuck with the good and the bad, forever and ever. No turning back. But when you are chosen to be a family member, they know your faults before you are invited to become a part of their family. They have accepted you just as you are. No questions asked!

I guess you could say that just as God chose me with unconditional love, so did James and Ann Kilpatrick. I always thought we just fit! It seemed Ann was meant to be my mom, and James was the only man I ever met after my dad died whom I admired enough to call Papa. My dad died when I was very young, so I just thought I was not meant to have a father figure in my life.

I never left their presence without James saying, "Call us now if you need us," and he never thought twice about saying, "Love you." Many times, when he became so sick, I would lean over and say, "I love you, Papa," and he never failed to say, "Love you, too." I will never forget the last time he was able to tell me that; he could only mouth the words slowly.

Papa was the most humble man I ever knew. He never thought he was worthy of the forgiveness the Heavenly Father had given him, the great family God had blessed him with, friends who would have given their lives for him, and a son (my little brother) and a daughter (me) who thought we were very blessed to have him in our lives. Oh, he wasn't perfect, but so close to it we just gave him the benefit of the doubt!

If I had to describe Papa in one word, it would be *gentle*. He had a gentleness about him that could capture the heart of a grown adult, a small child, or even an animal. Even a big, strong horse could sense the compassion Papa carried inside.

When my mom lay on her deathbed, Papa was going down fast and didn't feel like being there but he came anyway. On my mom's last night upon this earth, Ann kept trying to get Papa to go home, but time after time he would say, "No, let's stay a little longer." My birth mother died the next morning at 9:20, but God gave me a wonderful family to love me and really care about me. For that I am truly grateful. My little brother, Marty, and I even love each other like brother and sister.

Papa will always live in our family, because he left a part of himself in all of us. If he could talk to me now, he would say, "Wish you were here."

Love you Papa,
Patty Handley

Best cowboy to ever put on a hat and spurs.

Billy Kilpatrick

Our family honors James for defending us that night. I will always be grateful that he stood and fought for his family. It could have been a lot worse, but James put himself in harm's way to protect us. I loved him, and he will be missed.

Russell Kilpatrick

He was more than a brother; he was my best friend. I would have taken his pain. He was a man after God's own heart.

Harold Kilpatrick

James was a good man, and he always looked after me when I came home from school. He was the neatest person I have ever known. I loved him, and I miss him.

Faye Kilpatrick Simpson

I was close to James after Glenda and I got married. We bought a horse and didn't have a clue how to take care of it. James had much knowledge about horses, and he enjoyed sharing it. He was in his comfort zone with horses. He taught me everything I know about horses.

One day, we drove over to James and Ann's house. When we pulled up in the driveway, the horses were out in the front yard, grazing! They never tried to leave the yard. They knew their master, and they respected him. Glenda and I just stood there, amazed.

James Kilpatrick was the real deal.

Tiger Kilpatrick

I went to the radio broadcast every Sunday with my daddy, and every Sunday I would cry to go home with Uncle James. He would bring me a biscuit from Hardee's every Sunday morning. He also bought me a little red tricycle.

Uncle James and Aunt Ann would take me to the rodeos, and I was afraid of the clowns. I was also afraid of horses, but I would sit on the pony while Uncle James led it around. I felt safe with him. I loved him so much. He was very special to me.

Rachel Kilpatrick Golden

James Kilpatrick was a great man. He was in his element with horses. We got close during the years he was involved with the Sand Mountain Saddle Club. James helped us build an arena and got the horse shows started. He felt comfortable around his friends at the saddle club. I have never seen anyone do what he could with a horse, but he had a great teacher, his dad.

Donald Thomas

James had no fear of any animal. He would calmly walk up to the most high-spirited horse, look it in the eyes, and tell him who the boss was, and within minutes, he was leading that horse around like a puppy on a leash.

George Kilpatrick

He was a man's man and a man of his word. He should have been the Marlboro Man on the billboard. He was like a daddy to me, and I loved the man. He was always talking about his Lord. I will always miss him.

William Renfro

His life was an example to everyone who met him.

Jim Renfro

I knew James for thirty years, and we never had a cross word. He impressed me with his good heart and gentle ways. He was truly a man of God. I listened to his radio broadcast every Sunday morning. He was the best neighbor a man could have. When I got laid off, he gave me a job, and I will always be grateful for that.

Ronald Hayes

I met James Kilpatrick through the Sand Mountain Saddle Club. We shared many good times together. No one knew more about horses than James. He could look at a horse and tell you the age of the horse. If he told you a horse was sick and it was going to die, you might as well dig a hole.

James was my friend. When Parkinson's was taking over his body, Ann would drive him out to the house, and I would ride him around the farm on my gator. It hurt me to see him that way.

James Kilpatrick was a good man and a simple man.

I am very thankful for the time we spent together, and I miss him terribly.

Thomas Smith

It is hard to write about a man one considers to be an enigma, a man of few words, but nevertheless mesmerizing.

I remember James's hairstyle and how it reminded me of Audie Murphy's. His clothes were pressed to perfection, his boots were pointed and polished, and his belt buckles and cowboy hats were beautiful. To this day, I still love the cowboy look, and I myself still wear the boots and hats. I credit some of that influence to James, mixed with a little Roy Rogers and John Wayne. His twang also fascinated me. It was a cross between Appalachia and Southern drawl, with a dash of Texas twang melted over a little bluegrass vocal tone, and he was a good-looking man to boot. He seemed more like an uncle than a cousin by marriage.

The greatest thing about James Kilpatrick's life is how our Lord Jesus Christ transformed him. What a testimony! And it wasn't just a so-called "decision" for Christ but a true "born-again" soul who bore fruit from his true conversion to God's kingdom.

James had great patience with animals and children. It was evident in his years of leading ponies with children on their backs at our family reunions. He never complained about hosting the reunions, even though most of us never stayed to help clean up afterward.

I praise God for raising up a man like James Kilpatrick, who never sought the limelight for himself but lived to glorify the Lord and who understood as well as myself how God's amazing grace "saved a wretch like me." How wonderful that he has truly entered into his rest. Hallelujah!

"Precious in the sight of the Lord is the death of His saints" (Psalm 116:15). Amen

Denise R. Wilkes

James Kilpatrick reminded me of Conway Twitty; every hair was in place, and he was a spiffy dresser.

He was a unique person and a man of few words. He had wisdom learned not from books but from his own life experiences. If he had something to say, it was worth listening to. He was an honest man and a role model to many.

Children were drawn to James Kilpatrick, and he had a way with them. They would cling to him at the family reunions.

He reminded me of a horse whisperer. He had a way of communicating with them.

James went through some very hard times, but he came out as fine gold. God had brought him through a lot.

He was very special to our family, and we all miss him.

Yolanda Smith

I loved James Kilpatrick like a brother. He was always good to me and my girls. He was meant to be a part of our family. Ann Scott was the main ingredient in his life. He would not have been the man he was if not for Ann's influence on him. She was a constant, firm foundation in his life.

We loved him and miss him.

Erma Ragsdale

My name is Addie. Every third Sunday in May, there is an Amos family reunion at James and Ann's house. I have been attending these family reunions since I was a baby. When I was little, my favorite thing about the reunions was the horses. James would always let the children ride the horses. You could see the joy on the children's faces as he led them around on a horse. At one reunion, a baby colt had just

been born, and I was very excited! The best part was that James let me name the colt, so I decided to name it Coco. Coco was a beautiful horse, and I'm glad he let me name it. The picture that is included was taken when I was about three years old. I am riding Coco, and James is leading us. I miss you, James.

Addie Layne Morton

James Kilpatrick had much wisdom about a lot of things, especially horses. If he told you a horse was going to die, you might as well dig the grave, because the horse was going to die.

James already had Parkinson's when I joined the Cowboy Church and was baptized. James and Ann were there the day I got baptized, and it meant the world to me. Once a month, we would have Cowboys, Friends, and Fellowship. We would go to different homes or barns and have church and fellowship. We asked James if we could bring it to his house one month, and he obliged. I will never forget that day. Before the service started, James stood up and said, "If you're not a Christian, you need to be."

In one sentence, James Kilpatrick was the greatest man I have ever known, other than my father. If I had one more day with him, I would want to hang out with him and his horses. That was when he was at peace with himself and the world.

Tommy Baugh

I met James Kilpatrick when I was fifteen years old and had started to work in his cabinet shop. He was one of the finest men I've ever met, and he was one of a kind. He was honest, and he built on the foundation he was raised on, hard work and honesty.

James was a horseman, and what little I know about horses, I learned from him.

He had a pug-nosed bulldog named Spud who was as unique as James. One day, James and Spud were in the cabinet shop, spraying sanding sealer on some cabinets. I had been out running an errand, and when I came back and opened the door to the shop, the place was a fog, and James and Spud were high on fumes and looked ridiculously funny. James had a neighbor who picked up cans along the roadside. Spud would always bark and chase the man, and one day James whipped Spud for chasing him. Spud got his feelings hurt, ran away from home, and stayed gone all day. James was worried about him. Later that night, he came home, but he wouldn't have anything to do with James. When Spud was mad at him, he would turn his back to him. James treated him like he was a human being. The man had a way with animals and people.

Our family sings a song called "Sit Down and Rest a Little While," and James used to say, "We might sit down, but we won't have to rest, because we will have a new body that will never grow tired."

James Kilpatrick was my friend, and he always treated me with respect. I admired him, and I miss him. I was honored to know the man.

Tim Feemster

I came to know James Kilpatrick many years ago when I became his pastor. I quickly learned he was a man of commitment. He was committed to his church, his family, and his God. Shortly after becoming his pastor, I started hunting for a horse for my sons. I found them two horses, and James helped them learn how to ride and train them. We raised foals for several years, and James was always there to encourage the boys and answer any questions we had.

James always amazed me with his ability to deal with people and take people at their word. If you told James something, he did not want you to put it in writing to secure it; he just expected you to keep your word. And when he gave you his word, you could rest assured he would abide by whatever he said. His word was his bond!

While I was his pastor, my wife had problems with arthritis and was having trouble going up and down stairs in our home. I asked James about putting handrails up and where to get the materials. Soon after, James showed up at my house with handrails and everything needed to put them up. He put them up himself and would never tell me how much they cost. He was not one to speak out a lot, but if he knew someone needed something, he would be the first one to give.

My family will never forget the lessons James Kilpatrick taught us by his life. He was a quiet man who left behind a testimony that he pleased God.

Brother Harold Coe

7:30 a.m. Sunday Morning Radio Station

For many years, James was there Sunday after Sunday, as he went to the pulpit, sending the program out to everyone and a special message to the lost.

James loved to tell people about Jesus. He wanted the lost to come to Jesus.

James was a dedicated man, serving Jesus, determined to get the word out.

In the later years of his life, after being diagnosed with Parkinson's, he just kept on working for the Lord. I can still hear his hand trembling on the pulpit as he was starting the radio program, telling people about Jesus. James Kilpatrick loved people.

I believe James is in heaven, looking down and saying, "Get the word out to the lost."

James Kilpatrick, a great ambassador for Christ. I miss him.

Brother in Christ,
Billy Painter

Brother James Kilpatrick and I were and still are great friends, even though he has gone on to heaven in front of me. That does not change the fact that we are still friends. He is there waiting for us to come, and we are here waiting to go to where he is.

I have known James and Ann Kilpatrick since I was a little boy, and I always loved being around them. I remember when they got married.

I have a lot of memories of Brother James, but the best one is when he was saved by the grace of God.

Brother James was always a truthful and honest man, a man of character and integrity. He was a hardworking man who loved God, his family, and his church. Brother James was faithful in every way. He was a very humble man who had great compassion and love for everyone, especially children. He always carried a bag of candy or gum with him, and all the children knew that, so when they saw Brother James, they knew they had a treat coming.

He had a weekly radio program every Sunday morning in Boaz at WBSA radio station. He was faithful to this ministry for thirty-five years. The only time he missed a program was due to sickness. He helped an untold number of young and old preachers through this ministry. When a man announced his call to preach, Brother James would give him an appointment to preach. He loved preachers.

Brother James was a deacon at Bethlehem Baptist Church, where I pastor. I remember when the committee from our deacon body and I went to see Brother James about being ordained as a deacon. He was very humbled, and his reply was, "I am not worthy," but he was in the Lord. He accepted, and there were others ordained with him. Brother James was a man with a lot of wisdom, and it would do to listen to his advice. He not only had a ministry of sharing the Gospel, but he was an encourager. In our years together, he always prayed for me and encouraged me in my ministry. James Kilpatrick was to me what Barnabas was to Paul. Proverbs 25:11 says, "A word fitly spoken is like apples of gold in pictures of silver." Brother James seemed to always have the right word to speak to me. He was a man you could count on, a man who was not afraid to stand for what was right.

I can never say in words how much Brother James Kilpatrick, his dear wife, Ann, and their family, have enriched our lives. Not only did they enrich our lives, but they enriched the lives of so many other people as well. We will never know for sure how many lives James Kilpatrick influenced until that great and glad reunion day, when we shall be called home to glory. I praise the Lord for allowing our paths to cross in this life.

We shall be together again,
Wayne White
Pastor, Bethlehem Baptist Church

The man I called James Kilpatrick was a man's man. He was what the Bible describes as a meek man. Now, the thing about being meek is that it is badly misunderstood by most people, because it does not mean being a pushover or another word for being weak. *Meekness*, according to God's word, means power under control and gentleness in nature. Those of you who knew James will find it interesting that *meekness* was a term used for horses that were powerful but highly trained and submissive to their master. James was a master horseman who had a special touch with horses. He could simply look at a horse and within seconds be able to tell if the horse was of good quality or not. Most of all, James had been touched by the master, and he served the Lord with gladness.

One of my first memories of James took place in his barn when I was a teenager. A wild stallion he was training was throwing a fit in one of the stalls. It sounded as if the horse was going to tear down the barn. In all of the excitement, James walked up, went into the stall, and closed the door behind him. I asked my buddy Tim, "Is he crazy? He could get killed!" Tim replied, "Don't worry about James—worry about the horse!" I began to hear James speak to the horse like a little pony. I will never forget that.

James touched so many lives through his radio broadcast. Most of the people touched by his program were those who tuned in every Sunday morning for announcements, prayer requests, good Gospel singing, and solid Bible preaching. James's program touched me in a different way, because there was a time in my life when, because of failures and disobedience to God's will, I had quit preaching. In the winter of 2004, I made a strong rededication to the Lord Jesus Christ and renewed my commitment to preach and teach God's word in whatever capacity God willed for me. Brother James was one of the first to ask me to preach, and it was all I could do to keep from breaking down, because the enemy had convinced me that God couldn't use me. The second time Brother James asked me, I was overwhelmed, because I thought it would be a one-time deal; but over the next several years, he kept asking, and I kept going.

The thing that impressed me so with Brother James's life was the way he overcame so many obstacles and hurdles and became the man I knew. In life, when we absolutely hit rock-bottom, we have choices to make, and Brother James chose to get up, dust himself off, and keep on living. All I can say is, way to go, Brother James. He probably had some of the lowest lows in this life, but right now you can't get any higher than where he is. Job well done, Brother James.

Your friend,
Stephen White

James Kilpatrick was one of my best friends. He was a precious, honest man of God. James was genuinely concerned about humanity. My fondest memory of James is seeing him stand in front of the microphone at the radio station, begging people to come to know the Lord.
James was like E. F. Hutton; when he spoke, everyone listened. If he said something, it was worth listening to.
James touched me with his life, and he was always there for me. He had work to do here on Earth, and he did it well.
I had great respect for the man, and I miss him dearly.

Joe Southerland

James Kilpatrick was a true cowboy and a horseman. There was no horse or mule he couldn't handle. I spent a lot of time at the Kilpatrick farm growing up. James was buying and trading horses by the time he could ride one. He had a way with horses, but he also had a way with people.

He was an honest, simple man who loved the Lord. It was a blessing to know James Kilpatrick.

One of our last conversations was about horses.

Marlon Smith

I admired James Kilpatrick for his faith in God. He was an inspiration to many people. James was a man of integrity. He always showed me respect, and he called me Brother Wayne. He was a friend, and I enjoyed the time he helped us at the funeral home. He inspired me to help sponsor his radio broadcast, because he was a great supporter for the cause of Christ. He always gave the young preachers an opportunity to preach on the broadcast. I admired the way he treated and respected the ministers of God.

James made a difference in my life. He handled Parkinson's with a good attitude. My wife, Sue, always admired his hair, so I tried to comb mine like his.

I miss James Kilpatrick, my friend.

Brother Wayne Roden

I met James Kilpatrick when he and Ann worked at Carr Funeral Home in Boaz. I was in and out of there often. He always made sure there were peanuts available, because he knew how much I liked them. James would always bring me up to date on his horses.

James Kilpatrick's spirit of life was always uplifting. I will always cherish the few years I knew him.

Gaylon Dunn

James Kilpatrick had a heart of gold. I remember meeting him at Bethlehem Church. Each year at Vacation Bible School, James would bring ponies and lead them around and let the children ride. The man loved children and his horses.

I went to rodeos with James and Marty. James was one of those people you just like to be around.

I would go to his radio program on Sunday mornings, and I would always get under conviction. James Kilpatrick influenced my life in many ways. We all miss him.

Bart Kirtland

I worked for James and Ann Kilpatrick for seven years. When we first met, I thought his name was Jim, and I always called him Mr. Jim. He never did correct me on that, and as long as I worked for him, he was Mr. Jim. James was a patient man and a great teacher. He never scolded me when I messed up, but he would tenderly take me aside and show me a better way to do it.

James was a great influence in my life, and he always wanted to talk about the Lord and how blessed he was. He was an encourager, and he helped me through the years. I have great respect for the man. He was more than my boss; he was my friend.

JoAnn Kirtland

James and Ann Kilpatrick were my neighbors for several years. James was a very nice man who would help anyone in any way he could. I met James after he was diagnosed with Parkinson's, but he would still get up every day and walk over the farm to check on things. He would always stop by and check on my family to make sure we were doing okay. He loved children and would always bring my children candy and bubble gum. He also would lead the horses and let my children ride. They loved Mr. James.

James was enthusiastic, loyal, and hardworking. We miss him and know he is happy in heaven.

Tina Nuygen

ABOUT THE AUTHOR

Dana Hill began keeping a journal at the age of eighteen, after the death of her daddy in 1978. Journaling helped her in the healing process of dealing with and accepting the fact that dying is a part of living. For a born-again Christian, it is just passing from this life to our eternal life. Writing has been a hobby for Dana for the last thirty-two years.

After her son, Bobby, lost his best friend to cancer, Dana wrote and published "In the Shadow of His Cross," The Cliff Jacobs story. It is the witness and testimony of a young man battling cancer and how he endured through it all.

When the Kilpatrick family asked Dana to consider writing this book, she was honored and very humbled.

Dana works as a program secretary at First Baptist Church in Boaz, Alabama, and she and her husband are members of Bethlehem Baptist Church. She has a son, Bobby, who is a 2LT in the U.S. Army and is stationed at Fort Bragg, North Carolina, with the Eighty-Second Airborne. Dana has a daughter, Lori, who is a teacher at Shepherd's Place Christian School. Lori has two daughters, Anna and Abbie, and they bring much joy and happiness into their nana's life.

Dana and her husband, Larry, live a quiet, simple life in Sardis, Alabama.

"Writing is therapy for me, and being able to share the testimony of others and bring glory to God is a blessing." Dana Maria Hill